HOW TO CULTIVATE CONFIDENCE AND SELF-LOVE

HOW TO CULTIVATE CONFIDENCE AND SELF-LOVE

ULTIMATE TEEN GIRL'S GUIDE TO BOOSTING SELF-ESTEEM AND EMBRACING YOUR TRUE SELF (2-IN-1 COLLECTION)

ELLA BRADLEY

Teilingen
PRESS

Copyright © 2024 by Ella Bradley

All rights reserved. No part of this book may be reproduced, stored in a retrieval system, or transmitted in any form or by any means, electronic, mechanical, photocopying, recording, or otherwise, without the prior written permission of the publisher, Teilingen Press.

The information contained in this book is based on the author's personal experiences and research. While every effort has been made to ensure the accuracy of the information presented, the author and publisher cannot be held responsible for any errors or omissions.

This book is intended for general informational purposes only and is not a substitute for professional medical, legal, or financial advice. If you have specific questions about any medical, legal, or financial matters matters, you should consult with a qualified healthcare professional, attorney, or financial advisor.

Teilingen Press is not affiliated with any product or vendor mentioned in this book. The views expressed in this book are those of the author and do not necessarily reflect the views of Teilingen Press.

CONTENTS

Introduction   xi

HOW TO THRIVE IN YOUR TEENS

    Welcome to Your Journey   3
1. Navigating Friendships   13
2. Self-Care and Wellness   23
3. Navigating Puberty, Body and Emotional Changes   35
4. School and Academics   45
5. Your Digital World   57
6. Understanding Relationships   67
7. Facing Challenges   79
8. Expressing Yourself   89
9. Understanding Money   99
10. The World Around You   109
11. Career Exploration and Planning for the Future   119
    Your Story Continues   129

HOW TO EMBRACE YOUR SPARK

    Embracing Your Spark   139
1. Discovering Who You Are   149
2. Cultivating Positive Self-Talk   159
3. Building Healthy Relationships   171
4. Embracing Your Body   183
5. Finding Your Creative Side   193
6. Managing Stress and Anxiety   203
7. The Power of Resilience   217
8. Exploring Spirituality and Inner Peace   225
9. Speaking Up   235
10. Navigating Change   243
    Your Self-Love Journey   253

Epilogue	259
Your Feedback Matters	261
About the Author	263
Also by Ella Bradley	265

For my beautiful daughters.

To fall in love with yourself is the first secret to happiness.

ROBERT MORLEY

INTRODUCTION

Welcome to "How to Cultivate Confidence and Self-Love" an empowering 2-in-1 collection designed to guide you through the exhilarating, challenging, and utterly unique experience of being a teenage girl in today's modern world.

In the first part of this collection, "How to Thrive in Your Teens," we embark on an adventure to navigate the teenage years with confidence, resilience, and self-assurance. This book is a companion that walks you through understanding yourself, building lasting relationships, and setting ambitious goals. It's packed with practical advice on managing friendships, embracing your uniqueness, and planning for the future. It doesn't shy away from tough topics like bullying, failure, and loss, providing you with the tools you need to be a strong, self-aware woman.

In the second volume, "How to Embrace Your Spark," we dive deeper into the heart of self-love. This guide is your roadmap to turning self-doubt into self-love, encouraging you to become your biggest cheerleader and best version of yourself. Together, we'll

INTRODUCTION

explore the challenges of social pressures, body image, and finding your identity, offering ways to cultivate positive self-talk, build healthy relationships, and confidently embrace your body. This book is about learning to listen to your inner voice, fostering creativity, and navigating life's transitions with a curious and open mind.

This collection is a beacon of truth and empowerment in today's world, where teens are bombarded with mixed messages about who they should be. It's tailored to help you flourish during these transformative years, turning them into a period of growth, self-discovery, and self-love.

I hope this book will equip you with the knowledge, skills, and confidence to face the challenges of adolescence head-on. It's about helping you to understand that you are enough, just as you are, and encouraging you to embrace your true self with open arms.

Whether you're looking to boost your self-esteem, navigate the complexities of teenage life, or simply find a source of genuine self-love, "How to Cultivate Confidence and Self-Love" is your starting point.

Join me on this journey to discover the endless possibilities that come with embracing who you are and loving yourself unconditionally.

HOW TO THRIVE IN YOUR TEENS

A TEEN GIRL'S SURVIVAL GUIDE TO NAVIGATE ADOLESCENCE WITH CONFIDENCE, SELF-AWARENESS AND RESILIENCE

WELCOME TO YOUR JOURNEY

Stepping into your teenage years is like embarking on an epic adventure filled with discovery, challenges, and boundless opportunities. This journey is uniquely yours, and how you navigate it will shape not just your teenage years but the very essence of who you are becoming.

WELCOME TO YOUR JOURNEY

At the heart of this adventure is an important quest —the quest to understand yourself. This is not just about knowing your favorite color or whether you prefer movies over books; it's about diving deep into who you are. It's about recognizing your strengths and acknowledging your weaknesses. It's about understanding your emotions, thoughts, and reactions to the world around you.

Understanding yourself is like having a compass on this journey. It helps you make decisions that align with your true self. It guides you in forming relationships that are genuine and nurturing. It empowers you to embrace your uniqueness and to stand firm in your values and beliefs, even when the world seems to be pushing against you.

This quest is not without its challenges. There will be moments of doubt and confusion. There will be times when you question who you are and where you fit in this vast world. These moments are not setbacks, but part of the adventure. They are opportunities for you to grow, learn, and gain a deeper understanding of who you are.

Be kind to yourself as you embark on this quest to understand yourself. Allow yourself to make mistakes and dare to learn from them. Celebrate your wins, no matter how small they may seem. And most importantly, remember that understanding yourself is not a destination but a lifelong journey. With each step, you are uncovering more about the incredible person you are becoming.

So, take a deep breath, dear adventurer. The path to understanding yourself lies before you. It's time to take that first step with confidence, curiosity, and an open mind.

UNDERSTANDING YOURSELF

Understanding yourself involves delving into your identity and emotions, which are complex and ever-evolving. It requires courage, curiosity, and, most importantly, compassion towards yourself. As you navigate through the ups and downs of your teens, remember that self-discovery is not a destination but a continuous process.

In this phase of your life, your feelings and thoughts might seem like a whirlwind, constantly changing and evolving. This is perfectly normal. The teenage years are a time of profound growth, not just physically but emotionally and intellectually. You're beginning to form your own opinions, interests, and values, distinct from those of your family and friends. This process of differentiation is essential in developing your unique identity.

One of the first steps in understanding yourself is to acknowledge and accept your feelings, no matter how confusing or contradictory they may seem. It's okay to feel happy and sad at the same time, to be confident in some areas of your life while feeling insecure in others. These ups and downs are part of the human experience. Embracing your emotions without judgment creates a space for self-compassion and growth.

Another key aspect of self-understanding is recognizing what you're good at and what you can improve on. Everyone has a unique set of talents and abilities that make them special. You may be a great listener, a creative thinker, or a natural leader. Identifying these strengths can boost your self-esteem and guide you toward activities and careers that align with your passions and skills. At the same time, finding areas where you'd like to grow is equally important. Setting personal goals and challenges can help you develop resilience and perseverance, qualities that will serve you well throughout your life.

Self-reflection is a powerful tool in understanding yourself. It involves thinking about your experiences, choices, and reactions. Journaling can be a great way to practice self-reflection. Writing down your thoughts and feelings helps to clarify them, making it easier to identify patterns and triggers in your behavior. This self-awareness can lead to more mindful decision-making and a deeper understanding of your emotional needs.

Finally, understanding yourself is a journey that doesn't have to be undertaken alone. While it's about getting to know your inner world, sharing your thoughts and feelings with friends, family members, or mentors can provide valuable perspectives and support. These connections enrich your self-discovery process and remind you that you're not alone in your experiences.

As you continue on this path of self-understanding, be patient and kind to yourself. Growth takes time, and there will be moments of doubt and confusion. However, these challenges are not roadblocks but stepping stones, leading you toward a deeper, more meaningful understanding of who you are and who you dream to be.

BUILDING YOUR SUPPORT SYSTEM

As you step forward on this adventure of self-discovery and growth, it's essential to recognize that you don't have to do it alone. Building a solid support system is like constructing a safety net that catches you when you fall and a cheerleading squad that celebrates your victories, no matter how small. This network of trusted individuals can provide guidance, encouragement, and a listening ear when you need it most.

Who Makes Up Your Support System?

Your support system can include family members, friends, teachers, coaches, or anyone who positively influences your life. These people believe in you, even when you might not believe in yourself. They offer a shoulder to lean on during tough times and are there to share in your joys and successes. The quality of your support system matters more than the quantity. A few close, meaningful relationships can be far more beneficial than numerous superficial ones.

Cultivating Relationships

Building and maintaining these relationships requires effort and honesty. Be open to sharing your thoughts and feelings with them, and equally important, be a good listener. Showing appreciation for their support and returning it whenever possible will strengthen these bonds. A support system is a two-way street; it's about giving as much as receiving.

Seeking Mentors

In addition to friends and family, consider seeking mentors who can offer guidance and advice based on their experiences. A mentor could be a teacher who inspires you, a coach who pushes you to do better, or a professional in a field you're interested in. These relationships can provide invaluable insights and open doors to new opportunities.

Embracing Community Resources

Don't overlook the value of community resources. Libraries, community centers, and youth groups offer programs and workshops that can support your personal and academic growth. These spaces can also be great places to meet new people who share your interests and passions.

Navigating Challenges Together

Your support system is there for you through thick and thin. Don't be afraid to reach out for help when you're facing challenges. Whether it's stress from school, personal issues, or uncertainty about the future, talking about your problems with someone you trust can provide relief and lead to solutions. They can also offer perspectives and advice that you might not have considered.

A Foundation for Growth

As you continue exploring who you are and who you want to become, your support system will serve as a foundation for building your dreams and goals. They are your cheerleaders, sounding boards, and safety nets. Cherish these relationships, invest in them, and watch them enrich your life in ways you never imagined.

As you begin to set your sights on the future, remember that your support system is crucial to helping you achieve your goals and dreams. They provide the encouragement, advice, and reality checks needed to turn those dreams into actionable plans.

SETTING GOALS AND DREAMS

As you step into this exciting phase of your life, where every day feels like a new adventure waiting to unfold, it's essential to pause and think about what you wish to achieve. Setting goals and dreams is not just about scribbling down a list of things you hope to accomplish; it's about connecting with your deepest desires and aspirations, understanding what makes your heart sing, and creating a plan to make those dreams a reality.

Imagine your goals as seeds. Just as a seed needs the right environment, nourishment, and care to grow into a flourishing plant, your goals, too, require a nurturing environment, which includes a supportive community, positive affirmations, and a belief in your capabilities. But before you plant these seeds, you must understand what you wish to cultivate.

Start by asking yourself what brings you joy, fulfillment, and a sense of achievement. These questions might seem broad, but they're essential stepping stones. Your goals can range from academic achievements, like doing well in a subject that challenges you, to personal milestones, such as learning a new skill or hobby that excites you. There's no dream too big or too small. What matters is that it means something to you.

Once you've identified your goals, it's time to break them down into actionable steps. Think of this as creating a map for your journey. If your dream is to become a writer, your first steps might include setting aside time each day to write, reading books across different genres to expand your understanding, or even starting a blog to share your thoughts and refine your voice.

Breaking down your goals into smaller, manageable tasks makes the process less daunting and more achievable.

However, staying flexible and open to detours along the way is also important. Sometimes, the path to our dreams takes unexpected turns, and that's okay. These moments are not setbacks but opportunities to grow, learn, and discover new passions.

As you start setting goals and chasing dreams, celebrate your progress, learn from setbacks, and keep your eyes on the horizon. Your dreams are valid, your aspirations important, and with perseverance, a supportive community, and a belief in yourself, there's nothing you can't achieve.

So, take a deep breath, embrace the excitement of setting goals, and step forward with confidence into this beautiful journey of making your dreams a reality. This is your story, and you are the author.

EMBRACING CHANGE AND CHALLENGES

After setting your sights on the stars, it's time to step into reality. The path from where you are to where you want to be is rarely a straight line. It's filled with twists, turns, and many obstacles. But here's the secret: it's within these challenges that you find your true strength. Embracing change and challenges is not just about surviving; it's about thriving and discovering the depths of your potential.

Change is inevitable. Your dreams, goals, and interests might shift as you grow. This is a natural part of your journey. It's okay to outgrow what you once thought you wanted. Allow yourself the space to explore new pathways and interests. Every experience, whether it ends in success or learning, contributes to the person you are becoming.

Facing challenges, on the other hand, can feel daunting. It's like standing at the base of a mountain, looking up at the peak, wondering how you'll ever make it to the top. But every mountain is climbed one step at a time. Break down your challenges into smaller, manageable tasks. Celebrate each step forward, no matter how small, and learn from each setback.

One of the most powerful tools in your toolkit is your mindset. Approach each challenge with a growth mindset. Believe in learning, adapting, and growing from every situation. When you stumble, ask yourself, "What can I learn from this?" instead of focusing on the fall. This shift in attitude can transform obstacles into opportunities for growth. Feel free to reach out for help or advice. Sometimes, a fresh perspective is all you need to overcome a hurdle.

Embracing change and challenges is both an external and internal journey. Nurture your body, mind, and spirit. Practice self-care, stay connected with your emotions, and never underestimate the power of a good night's sleep. Your well-being is the foundation upon which you can build your dreams.

Every change and challenge is an opportunity to grow stronger, wiser, and closer to the person you dream to be. Your story is unique; every step, even the difficult ones, is part of your story. Embrace it all with courage, grace, and a heart full of dreams.

CHAPTER SUMMARY

- This book will help you embark on the journey of self-discovery and personal growth during your teenage years. Throughout it, you'll learn the importance of

understanding yourself, including recognizing your strengths, weaknesses, and emotions, and using this to navigate life's challenges.
- Self-discovery is a continuous process that involves self-reflection, embracing your emotions, and setting personal goals.
- Building a strong support system of family, friends, mentors, and community resources is important for personal development and overcoming challenges.
- Set goals and dreams by connecting with your deepest desires and aspirations and breaking them down into actionable steps.
- Remain open to change, because the path to achieving your dreams may involve unexpected detours and opportunities for growth.
- Embracing challenges is an opportunity to discover your true strength, resilience, and potential, with a growth mindset being a powerful tool.
- Self-care and strong community support are foundational for successfully navigating the journey of personal growth and achieving your dreams.

CHAPTER 1
NAVIGATING FRIENDSHIPS

Friendships, much like the seasons, change and evolve. During your teenage years, you'll find that making and keeping friends can be both a source of joy and a challenge. The art of friendship is not just about finding people who share your interests or make you laugh; it's also about building and nurturing respectful, supportive, and understanding relationships.

Making friends starts with being open to new connections. Remember, everyone is seeking that sense of belonging, just like you. Be the person who smiles first, asks questions, and shows genuine interest in others. Join clubs, teams, or groups that align with your interests. These extracurricular activities are opportunities to meet like-minded individuals who share your passions.

However, making friends is just the beginning. Keeping them requires effort, empathy, and communication. Be the friend you wish to have. Show up for your friends, not just during the fun times but especially during the tough ones. Listen to them with an open heart and without judgment. Celebrate their successes as if they were your own and offer your shoulder during their times of need.

Communication is the foundation of any strong friendship. Be honest but kind with your words. It's not just about what you say but how you say it. Misunderstandings are inevitable, but they can be resolved with patience and openness. Learn to express your feelings and needs clearly, and equally important, learn to listen. Sometimes, being a good friend means understanding what is left unsaid.

Respect boundaries, both yours and theirs. Every friendship is unique, and understanding each other's limits and comfort zones is crucial. This mutual respect builds trust, and trust is the foundation upon which lasting friendships are built.

Lastly, know that it's okay to outgrow friendships. People change, and sometimes, the friendships that once felt perfect no longer fit. It's a natural part of life. Cherish the memories and lessons learned from these relationships, and know that new friendships are just around the corner.

In navigating the complex world of friendships, know that your most important relationship is with yourself. You must be open to the possibility of making and keeping friends to let true friendships blossom.

HOW TO DEAL WITH CONFLICTS

Friendships are the threads that add color and warmth to the experiences of your teens. But, like any relationship, misunderstandings and conflicts can occur. It's an inevitable part of growing up, but dealing with these disagreements can feel as scary as navigating a labyrinth. However, with the right approach, resolving conflicts can strengthen the bonds of friendship, teaching invaluable lessons about empathy, understanding, and communication.

First and foremost, recognize that uncomfortable conflicts are not the end of the world. They are, in fact, opportunities for growth. When a disagreement arises, take a step back and breathe. Reacting in the heat of the moment can escalate the situation, so give yourself time to cool down and collect your thoughts.

Once you're in a calmer state of mind, try to see the situation from your friend's perspective. Empathy is a powerful tool. It helps you understand their feelings and motivations, which might not be apparent at first. There's always more to the story than your viewpoint.

Communication is the bridge that connects misunderstanding to understanding. Approach your friend to listen and be heard. Choose a time and place you feel comfortable and won't be interrupted. Use "I" statements to express how you feel without placing blame. For example, instead of saying, "You always ignore me," try, "I feel hurt when I don't get a response from you." This way, you're taking responsibility for your feelings and inviting your friend to share theirs without putting them on the defensive.

Listening is just as crucial as speaking. When your friend shares their side, listen to understand, not reply. Avoid interrupting or planning your response while they're talking. Acknowledge their feelings and show that you value their perspective, even if you don't agree with everything they say.

Finding a resolution might not happen immediately, and that's okay. Some conflicts require time to work through. The key is to keep the lines of communication open and to approach the situation with patience and an open heart. Your friendship might be the same as before. Still, sometimes, friendships evolve into something deeper and more meaningful after overcoming challenges together.

Know that it's okay to agree to disagree. Not all conflicts have a clear resolution; sometimes, the best outcome is respecting each other's differences. The goal is not to win an argument but to maintain a friendship that's important to both of you.

Lastly, know when to seek help. If a conflict escalates beyond what you can handle, involves bullying or harassment, or makes you feel uncomfortable, it's crucial to reach out to a trusted adult for guidance. There's no shame in asking for help when the situation calls for it.

Navigating the stormy waters of friendship conflicts is difficult, but it teaches us resilience, empathy, and the art of communication. These skills are not just valuable in maintaining friendships; they're essential for all relationships in life. So, embrace these challenges as they come, knowing that each is an opportunity to grow stronger, both as an individual and a friend.

HOW TO DEAL WITH PEER PRESSURE

Navigating friendships as a teenager is like riding a bike on a winding path. You must handle peer pressure by knowing when you're being led off your path and learning how to steer yourself back to where you want to go.

Peer pressure is the influence a peer group exerts in encouraging a person to change their attitudes, values, or behaviors to follow group norms. It's a powerful force, and while not always negative, it's important to understand its dynamics to navigate it effectively.

Imagine you're at a party, and someone offers you a drink or a cigarette, saying, "Everyone's doing it." That's peer pressure. It's the nudge to do something because it seems like the norm within your group or the broader social circle. It's not just about risky behaviors, though. Peer pressure can push you towards positive actions, like joining a study group or volunteering, but it can also lead you away from your true self.

The key to dealing with peer pressure is knowing yourself. What are your values? What do you stand for? A strong sense of self makes you less likely to follow the crowd. It's like having a map while riding your bike on that winding path; you know where you're headed no matter which way the path turns.

Another approach you can take to reduce the influence of peer pressure is to choose your friends wisely. Surround yourself with people who respect you and your choices, friends who uplift rather than undermine. True friends will never pressure you to do something that makes you uncomfortable or goes against your values. They'll ride alongside you, even if you're headed in different directions.

Learning to say "no" is also a crucial skill. It's about knowing when to assert your boundaries. Practice saying "no" in a firm yet polite way. You don't owe anyone an explanation for your choices, but if you feel like giving one, keep it simple and honest. Saying "no" to something you don't want to do is saying "yes" to yourself and your well-being.

You can be a positive influence on your friends, too. Peer pressure works both ways, and you have the power to be a force for good among your friends. Encourage kindness, respect, and authenticity. By being true to yourself and supporting others in doing the same, you contribute to a culture where everyone feels free to be their best selves.

Understanding peer pressure is about recognizing what it looks like and learning to navigate it with confidence. It's about making choices that are right for you, even when they go against the status quo. Don't forget that it's okay to seek guidance from adults or friends when you need help figuring out what to do. You're not alone; with time, you'll become skilled at navigating the path of friendships, steering yourself towards a life that's truly your own.

THE POWER OF EMPATHY

Empathy is the ability to understand and share the feelings of another. Empathy is a superpower for friendships, especially during your teenage years. It's what connects us, allowing us to build deeper, more meaningful relationships. But how do you harness this power, and why is it so important in navigating the complex world of friendships?

Firstly, empathy lets you see the world from your friend's perspective. Imagine you're in their shoes, feeling what they feel, whether it's joy, sadness, or frustration. This doesn't mean you must agree with everything they say or do. Instead, it's about acknowledging their feelings as valid and trying to understand where they're coming from. This understanding is the foundation of any strong friendship. It builds trust and a sense of safety, where both of you feel seen and heard.

Practicing empathy also helps in resolving conflicts. Disagreements are natural in any relationship, but they don't have to lead to lasting fights. When you approach a conflict with empathy, you're more likely to find a resolution that respects everyone's feelings and needs. It's about listening actively without immediately jumping to defend your point of view. Often, we're so focused on getting our point across that we forget to listen. But when we truly listen, we open the door to solutions that might not have been apparent in the heat of the moment.

Empathy encourages a deeper connection and loyalty among friends. It's comforting to know that someone will try to understand you, even when you're at your worst. This doesn't mean you should tolerate toxic behavior. Instead, it's about supporting each other through thick and thin, celebrating the highs, and offering a shoulder during the lows. These are the friendships that stand the test of time.

So, how can you practice empathy? Start by being curious about your friends' experiences and feelings. Ask open-ended questions and listen to their answers. Try to avoid judgment, even if their perspective vastly differs from yours. Empathy is not about solving their problems but about being present and offering support.

Empathy is also about recognizing your emotions and how they influence your reactions. This self-awareness can help you navigate not just your friendships but also all your relationships more effectively. It allows you to communicate more clearly and avoid misunderstandings leading to unnecessary conflict.

In essence, empathy is the glue that holds friendships together. It allows you to build stronger, more meaningful connections and navigate the ups and downs of teenage relationships. By practicing empathy, you're not just being a better friend but also setting the stage for healthier, more fulfilling relationships throughout your life.

SAYING GOODBYE TO FRIENDSHIPS

As with everything in life, when it comes to friendships, there may be a time when you must face the bittersweet reality of saying goodbye. Many of us wish we could skip it, but it's also a crucial part of growing and learning about ourselves and the world around us. Letting go of a friendship doesn't mean you've failed. Instead, it shows that you're evolving, and sometimes, our paths diverge from those we once walked alongside.

Saying goodbye to a friendship can happen for various reasons. Perhaps you've grown apart, your interests have changed, or a situation occurred that you can't move past. Regardless of the reason, we can approach this goodbye with the same empathy and understanding we cherish in our connections.

First, acknowledge your feelings. It's okay to feel sad, confused, or even relieved. These emotions are all part of the process, and recognizing them allows you to begin healing. It's important to permit yourself to grieve the loss of what once was.

Communication is vital, even in goodbyes. Have an honest conversation with your friend about your decision. This isn't about placing blame but expressing your feelings and providing closure for both of you. It's a sign of respect for what you've shared and a step towards understanding.

In some cases, a direct conversation might not be possible or healthy. Finding a way to say goodbye in your heart is also okay if that's the situation. Write a letter you never send, journal about your memories, or have a symbolic goodbye, like planting a flower or releasing a balloon. It's about finding closure in a way that feels right to you.

Remember to carry the lessons and happy memories with you as you move on. Every friendship, no matter how it ends, teaches us something valuable about love, resilience, and the importance of connection. It's okay to cherish the good times even as you let go.

Finally, be open to the new friendships that await you. Saying goodbye to one friend doesn't mean closing the door on future connections. It's simply a step towards discovering new people who will walk with you in the years to come.

Letting go is never easy, but it shows our ability to grow and change. As you experience this challenging but necessary part of life, remember you're not alone. Every goodbye carries the promise of a new hello; with each step, you're becoming more of the person you're meant to be.

CHAPTER SUMMARY

- Friendships evolve, and they require effort, empathy, and communication to maintain.
- Making friends involves being open to new connections and joining groups that align with your interests.

- Keeping friends requires showing up for them, listening without judgment, and respecting boundaries.
- Communication, honesty, and understanding are key to resolving conflicts and misunderstandings in friendships.
- Dealing with peer pressure involves knowing yourself, choosing friends wisely, and learning to say "no."
- Empathy is crucial in friendships, allowing for deeper connections and helping resolve conflicts.
- Saying goodbye to friendships is a part of growth, and it's important to approach farewells with empathy and openness to future connections.
- It's natural to outgrow friendships; cherishing memories and lessons learned is part of moving forward.

CHAPTER 2
SELF-CARE AND WELLNESS

Understanding and prioritizing your health is not just about the physical aspect but also your mental and emotional well-being. Self-care is about recognizing that your health is a multifaceted treasure; all its dimensions deserve care and attention. As you go through life, it's important to remember that taking care of your mind is as important as taking care of your body.

Mental health is the foundation of your overall well-being. It influences how you think, feel, and behave daily. It affects your ability to cope with stress, overcome challenges, build relationships, and recover from life's setbacks and hardships. Good mental well-being allows you to realize your full potential, work productively, and make meaningful contributions to your community.

So, how do you prioritize your mental health? First, it's about creating a safe space within yourself and your environment. This means fostering a positive mindset, where self-compassion and kindness are your guiding principles. Understand that it's okay not to be okay and that seeking help is a sign of strength, not weakness.

Another way to strengthen your mental wellness is to develop a routine that includes activities you love and that make you feel good. Whether reading, painting, dancing, or spending time in nature, these activities can provide a much-needed escape, reduce stress, and boost your mood and self-esteem.

Keeping your feelings bottled up can lead to increased stress and feelings of isolation. Find trusted friends, family members, or professionals to talk to about what you're going through. Sharing your thoughts and feelings can be incredibly freeing and essential to managing your mental health.

Be mindful of your digital well-being. In a world where social media can distort perceptions of reality, taking breaks from the screen and engaging in real-life connections is important. Comparing your situation to someone else's highlight reel can be detrimental to your mental health. Focus on your journey, knowing that everyone's path is unique.

Prioritizing your health means embracing a holistic approach to self-care, where your mental, emotional, and physical well-being are interconnected and equally important. When you take steps to care for your mind, you're setting the foundation for a healthier, happier you. Your mental health matters, and it's okay to reach out for help when you need it.

MENTAL HEALTH MATTERS

In the whirlwind of your teenage years, amidst the demands of school, extracurricular activities, and social life, it's easy to let your mental health slip to the back burner. But as we discovered earlier, your mental well-being is as crucial as your physical health. It allows you to build your dreams, face challenges, and cultivate resilience. So, let's dive into why mental health matters and how you can nurture it with the same dedication you give to other aspects of your life.

Society often paints a picture of adolescence filled with endless fun and discovery, but the reality can be quite different. It's okay not to be okay. You might face pressures from various parts of life - academic, social, or even from yourself. It's normal to feel overwhelmed, anxious, or down at times. Recognizing these feelings and accepting them as part of your journey is the first step toward managing your mental health.

You don't have to carry your burdens alone. Sharing your thoughts and feelings can give you different perspectives, valuable advice, and the comforting realization that many people are willing to support you. Talking about what you're going through can be incredibly freeing, whether with friends, family, or a professional. It's like untying a knot inside your chest.

Developing a self-care routine is another way you can boost

your mental health. Self-care isn't just about bubble baths and face masks; it's about doing things that genuinely make you feel good and at peace. It could be reading, painting, playing an instrument, or walking in nature. These activities aren't superficial; they're essential for your mental well-being. They allow you to recharge, find joy in the little things, and give you a break from the demands of daily life.

Mindfulness and meditation have also proven to be practical tools for managing stress and anxiety. Taking a few minutes each day to sit quietly, breathe deeply, and be present can significantly reduce feelings of anxiety and improve your overall mood. There are plenty of apps and online resources to guide you if you're new to meditation.

Lastly, never underestimate the power of a good night's sleep. This is the topic of the next section, it's worth exploring due to its profound impact on mental health. Sleep is when your body and mind recover from the day's stresses. Ensuring you get enough rest is crucial for your emotional and psychological well-being.

Your mental health matters, not just for surviving your teenage years but for thriving in them. There will be ups and downs, but you can navigate the challenges and emerge stronger with the right tools and support.

THE IMPORTANCE OF SLEEP

When you're busy spending your days studying, socializing, and perhaps even starting your first job, it's easy to let something as fundamental as sleep slip down your list of priorities. Yet, embracing the power of a good night's rest is one of the most transformative habits you can adopt for your overall well-being.

Sleep isn't just a pause from your daily activities; it's a critical period of restoration for your body and mind. During these precious hours, your body repairs itself, your brain consolidates memories, and your emotions get a much-needed reset. Think of it as your body's way of tidying up, ensuring you're ready to face another day with energy and clarity.

For many teens, the challenge in getting enough sleep often lies in balancing the desire to stay up late with the need to rise early for school. This mismatch between social habits and biological needs can lead to a sleep deficit, which can have ripple effects on your health over time. Not getting enough sleep can impair cognitive functions, making learning and concentration more difficult. It can also affect your mood, leading to irritability or sadness, weakening your immune system, making you more susceptible to illnesses.

So, how can you ensure that sleep becomes a non-negotiable part of your self-care routine? Start by creating a sleep-friendly environment. This means making your bedroom a sanctuary for rest. Consider the comfort of your bed, the temperature of the room, and the amount of light filtering in. A cool, dark, and quiet space can significantly enhance the quality of your sleep.

Next, establish a consistent bedtime routine. This could involve winding down for 30 minutes before sleep by reading a book, taking a warm bath, or practicing gentle yoga or meditation. The key is to signal to your body that it's time to shift gears from the hustle and bustle of the day to a more relaxed state.

It's also important to be mindful of your screen time in the evening. The blue light emitted by phones, tablets, and computers can interfere with your body's natural sleep-wake cycle, making it harder to fall asleep. Try setting a digital curfew for yourself, for example by aiming to stop using your devices at least an hour before bed.

Lastly, aim for consistency in your sleep schedule. Going to bed and waking up at the same time every day, even on weekends, can help regulate your body's internal clock, making it easier to fall asleep and wake up naturally.

Incorporating these practices into your life might not happen overnight, and that's okay. The goal is to gradually build habits that support your sleep, recognizing its vital role in your path to becoming the best version of yourself. Taking care of your body through proper rest is as important as nourishing it with good food and keeping it active. Together, these pillars of self-care form the base for building a healthy, happy, and fulfilling life.

NUTRITION AND EXERCISE

After understanding sleep's crucial role in your overall well-being, it's time to dive into another essential pillar of self-care: nutrition and exercise. These two components are your body's fuel and maintenance, ensuring you're not just awake but energized and thriving.

Nutrition: Your Body's Best Friend

Think of your body as a high-performance vehicle. Just as you wouldn't fill a sports car with the wrong type of fuel, feeding your body with nutritious foods is key to ensuring it runs smoothly. But don't worry, this isn't about strict diets or depriving yourself of the foods you love. It's about balance and making informed choices.

Start by incorporating more fruits and vegetables into your meals. They're packed with the vitamins and minerals your body craves for energy and health. If you're not a big fan of veggies, try sneaking them into smoothies or experimenting with different cooking methods. You might be surprised by what you end up liking!

Next, pay attention to hydration. Drinking enough water throughout the day can improve your skin, energy levels, and overall function. If water is too bland, add a slice of lemon or cucumber for a refreshing twist.

Lastly, listen to your body. It's okay to indulge in your favorite treats occasionally. The key is moderation and understanding that food is not just fuel but also a source of enjoyment.

Exercise: More Than Just Moving

Exercise isn't just about losing weight or building muscle; it's about respecting and appreciating what your body can do. Exercise releases endorphins, which are natural mood lifters, helping to reduce stress and anxiety. Finding an activity you love can make exercise feel less like a chore and more like a fun part of your day. It can also provide a welcome break from study and work commitments.

You don't have to commit to a rigorous workout schedule to experience the benefits of exercise. Start small with activities like walking, dancing in your room, or trying out yoga. The goal is to move your body in ways that feel good and bring you joy.

Once you've found activities you enjoy, try incorporating exercise into your weekly routine. For example, you could find three to four days a week to exercise that fits around your school, hobbies, and social activities, aiming for at least 30 minutes of physical activity on these days.

Exercise is a celebration of what your body can do, not a punishment for what you ate. It's about building strength, flexibility, and resilience physically and mentally.

Just as nutrition and exercise can nourish your body, finding peace and tranquility through meditation and mindfulness will nourish your soul. It's all about finding the right balance that works for you, allowing you to live your best life.

FINDING YOUR ZEN

After focusing on the physical aspects of your well-being through nutrition and exercise, it's equally important to turn our attention inward to our mental and emotional health. Finding your zen means discovering peace, balance, and joy in your daily life, especially during the rollercoaster years of your teens. This process is deeply personal and can look different for everyone, but the following universal practices can help guide you to a calmer state of mind.

Mindfulness and Meditation

One of the most effective ways to find your zen is through mindfulness and meditation. Mindfulness is about living in the moment and focusing on your current experience rather than dwelling on the past or worrying about the future. It can be as simple as paying full attention to your breathing, the sensations in your body, or the sounds around you. Meditation, a practice that often incorporates mindfulness, involves sitting quietly and focusing your mind for a period of time. You don't need any special equipment or a lot of time; just a few minutes each day can significantly affect your stress levels and overall mood.

Journaling

Writing down your thoughts and feelings can be a powerful way to process emotions and gain clarity. Whether grappling with a difficult decision, celebrating a success, or simply documenting your day-to-day experiences, journaling provides a safe space for self-expression. It can also be an excellent tool for setting goals and reflecting on personal growth.

Connecting with Nature

Spending time in nature has been shown to reduce stress, enhance mood, and improve mental health. Whether it's a walk in the park, a hike in the woods, or just sitting outside and soaking in the surroundings, connecting with the natural world can help you feel more grounded and at peace.

Creative Outlets

Creative expression is another fantastic way to find your zen. Whether you love drawing, painting, writing, dancing, playing an instrument, or any other creative expression, these activities can be incredibly therapeutic. They allow you to channel your emotions into something tangible and can be a source of joy and satisfaction.

Your Support System

Finally, finding your zen is not just an individual journey; it's also about the people you surround yourself with. As we explored earlier in this book, building a solid support system of friends, family, and mentors who understand and encourage you can make all the difference. These relationships provide comfort, advice, and a sense of belonging, helping you navigate the challenges of teenage life with confidence and resilience.

Finding your zen is a personal journey that takes time and patience. There's no right or wrong way to go about it; what works for someone else might not work for you. The key is to explore different practices and activities until you find what brings you peace and joy. You're setting yourself up for a healthy, balanced life by taking care of your mental and emotional well-being.

CHAPTER SUMMARY

- Self-care and wellness encompass physical health and mental and emotional well-being, emphasizing the importance of caring for the mind and body.
- Mental health is crucial for daily functioning, influencing your thoughts, feelings, behaviors, and ability to cope with stress and challenges. Prioritizing your mental health involves creating a positive mindset, fostering self-compassion, engaging in enjoyable activities, and openly communicating feelings.
- Digital well-being is important, and taking breaks from social media and screen time can help you foster real-life connections and avoid negative comparisons.

- Sleep is a powerful and transformative habit for overall well-being, with adequate rest supporting cognitive functions, mood regulation, and immune system health.
- Nutrition and exercise are essential pillars of self-care, with balanced eating and physical activity contributing to energy, health, and enjoyment of life.
- Finding peace and tranquility through mindfulness, meditation, journaling, connecting with nature, and creative expression can help you strengthen your mental and emotional health.
- Building a trusted support system of friends, family, and mentors can help you navigate the challenges of teenage life with confidence and resilience.

CHAPTER 3
NAVIGATING PUBERTY, BODY AND EMOTIONAL CHANGES

This chapter is your companion through the twists and turns of puberty, a phase of your teens that might seem overwhelming but is filled with growth, discovery, and transformation.

Puberty is like the official welcome party to your teenage years, but instead of balloons and cake, you're greeted with hormones and growth spurts. It's the period when your body starts to develop from a child into an adult, caused by a change in hormones that leads to a series of physical and emotional changes within you.

So, what's happening behind the scenes? It all begins in your brain, with the pituitary gland sending signals to your body to start producing hormones like estrogen and testosterone. These hormones are responsible for all the changes you'll experience during this time.

The timeline for this transformation varies widely. Some girls might start noticing changes as early as eight years old, while others might not until they're fourteen. How your body changes and at what pace during puberty will be unique to you.

As you progress through puberty, you'll grow taller, your hips will widen, and you'll develop breasts. You'll also notice hair growing in new places and changes to your skin and voice. It may seem like a lot, but it's all perfectly normal and every girl will go through it.

Understanding puberty is the first step in embracing the changes your body is going through. It's a sign that you're growing up, and with that comes a new level of independence and responsibility. Puberty isn't a race. It's a phase of life that unfolds differently for everyone, and there's no right or wrong way to go through it. So, as you step into this new chapter, do so with confidence and curiosity.

PHYSICAL CHANGES

During puberty, your body becomes a canvas for change, painting a picture of the unique woman you're becoming. These physical transformations are like milestones on the road to adulthood, each marking a new chapter in your story.

First, let's talk about growth spurts. Over time, your jeans might feel like they've shrunk in the wash, but in reality, you're growing. This increase in height is one of the first signs of puberty, making you reach for the top shelf with newfound ease. Like a sunflower reaching for the sun, everyone grows at their own pace.

The development of breasts often comes with mixed emotions. From budding breasts to buying your first bra, these changes can feel exciting and awkward at the same time. Feeling self-conscious, curious, anxious, or even indifferent about these changes is normal. And if you find yourself comparing your body to others, remember that every person's journey is as unique as their fingerprint. Breasts come in all shapes and sizes and don't follow a one-size-fits-all timeline.

As your body evolves, you'll also notice hair sprouting in places it wasn't before—under your arms, on your legs, and around your pubic area. This new hair growth is completely natural. There's nothing wrong with body hair, and it marks another step in your progress through puberty. How you manage it—letting it grow, shaving, or waxing—is entirely up to you. Your body, your choice.

Then there's the changes to your skin. The joys of puberty can sometimes bring about acne and oily skin, thanks to those active hormones in your body. While it might feel like your skin is rebelling against you, know that with a good skincare routine and patience, this too will pass.

Dealing with pimples during your teenage years involves a combination of good skincare habits and lifestyle adjustments. Start with a gentle skincare routine: wash your face twice daily with a mild cleanser to remove excess oil and dirt, and avoid harsh scrubbing, which can irritate the skin further. Moisturize with a non-comedogenic product to keep your skin hydrated without clogging pores. Stay hydrated and get enough sleep, as stress and fatigue can trigger breakouts. If your acne persists or worsens, consider consulting a dermatologist for personalized advice and treatment options, which may include prescription medications. Patience and consistency with your routine are key, as improvements in acne can take several weeks to become visible. Remember that these skin imperfections don't define your beauty or worth.

Lastly, you might notice your voice changing. It might not be as dramatic as the voice changes that boys experience, but it's part of your body's way of saying, "Hey, I'm growing up!"

As your body changes, so do your hygiene needs. You may need to shower more often, use deodorant, or change your skincare routine to meet your body's new demands. Establishing good hygiene habits now will keep you feeling fresh and confident and help prevent issues like acne or body odor.

Navigating these physical changes can feel like a rollercoaster ride—one minute, you're up, the next, you're down. But through it all, embrace your body's evolution with kindness and patience. These changes are the physical signs of the incredible process happening within, transforming you into the amazing woman you're meant to become. So, stand tall, embrace the changes, and know you're not alone.

ALL ABOUT PERIODS

Welcome to the topic every girl has questions about: Periods. Think of it as your body's monthly report card, saying, "Hey, everything's working as it should!" It might seem a bit scary at first, with all the talk about cycles and pads and cramps, but it's just another part of the incredible journey your body is on.

Menstruation, or your period, is your body's way of shedding the lining of the uterus when there's no pregnancy. It's a sign that your body is capable of creating life, which, when you think about it, is amazing. The length of a period is different for everyone; it can last anywhere from a few days up to a week.

Your period is just one part of your menstrual cycle, which starts with menstruation and ends when your next period begins. It usually lasts between 28 to 35 days, but it can be shorter or longer, especially in the first few years. The cycle is like your body's monthly planner. It is regulated by hormones like estrogen and progesterone, which control the release of an egg and the preparation of your uterus for potential pregnancy.

There are many different options you have for managing your period. Finding the right product is all about what makes you feel comfortable and secure. Pads are a straightforward choice—soft and absorbent, they stick to your underwear and catch blood externally. Tampons are small, absorbent cylinders you insert into your vagina; they can feel a bit odd at first but allow for more physical freedom. Menstrual cups are flexible cups made from silicone or rubber that you insert into your vagina to collect blood; they're reusable and eco-friendly once you learn how to use them comfortably. Period underwear looks like regular underwear but has a special layer to absorb period blood; they're an easy and reliable option for those who want hassle-free protection. If you're expecting your period or don't know when it's coming, it's a good idea to carry a pad or tampon in your bag so you're ready in case of an emergency.

Cramps are a common part of your menstrual cycle that can vary from being slightly bothersome to quite painful. They are caused during your period when your uterus contracts to help shed its lining. To help soothe the discomfort, you can use heat pads, do some light exercise, or take pain relief medication. It's essential to pay attention to what your body needs during this time.

Tracking your period can help you predict when your period will arrive and notice any changes in your cycle. It's like keeping a diary for your body. It can be as simple as marking when you have your period on a calendar or using one of the many apps available.

Understanding your menstrual cycle is empowering. It's about getting to know your body and its rhythms. While there might be moments of inconvenience and discomfort, your period is a powerful reminder of the incredible things your body can do.

EMOTIONAL AND MENTAL CHANGES

As you navigate the ups and downs of puberty, you'll notice it's not just your body that's riding the waves of change—your emotions and mental state are on their own rollercoaster, too.

During puberty, your brain undergoes significant development. This can make your emotions feel more intense and overwhelming. You might be laughing one minute, and the next, you could find yourself tearing up over a commercial. It's all part of puberty, and it's completely normal.

These emotional fluctuations are partly due to hormones, those chemical messengers in your body responsible for the physical changes you're experiencing. Just like they're causing changes to your body, they're tweaking your emotions, too. This can lead to mood swings, where you feel like you're on an emotional pendulum, swinging from happy to sad to irritable and back again.

Developing a healthy body image during this time can be challenging, especially with the impact of social media, which can paint unrealistic pictures of perfection. Your body is your lifelong home, and it's going through many changes right now. Treat it with kindness and respect, and try to silence those critical voices, both from within and from the outside world. Celebrate what your body can do rather than focusing on how it looks.

Navigating new feelings and attractions is another part of the emotional aspect of puberty. You may see your peers in a different light, developing crushes or deeper friendships. It's an exciting time, but it can also be confusing. There's no rush to figure everything out. Let your feelings unfold naturally, and always stay true to yourself.

Stress and anxiety might also knock on your door more often during these years. Developing healthy coping strategies is important, like talking to someone you trust, engaging in activities you enjoy, or practicing mindfulness and relaxation techniques.

Everyone's experience is unique, but we all walk the path of growing up. Embrace the changes, lean on your support system, and remember, this chapter of your life is about discovering who you are and want to become.

HOW AND WHEN TO SEEK HELP

As you navigate the landscape of puberty, with its peaks of joy and valleys of challenge, it's important to recognize when you need a helping hand. This section is your guide to understanding when and how to seek support, reminding you that reaching out is a sign of strength, not weakness.

While many aspects of puberty are universal, your experience is uniquely yours. If you feel overwhelmed by physical changes that seem too intense or different from what your peers are experiencing, it might be time to talk to a healthcare professional. This includes concerns about your menstrual cycle, such as periods that are too heavy, too painful, or irregular in a way that disrupts your daily life.

Emotionally and mentally, puberty can sometimes feel like a stormy sea. If you struggle to navigate these waters, feeling constantly sad, anxious, or irritable, it's important to reach out. Mental health is just as important as physical health, and there are people ready and willing to support you. This could be a trusted adult, a school counselor, or a mental health professional.

Asking for help is a brave and proactive step toward caring for yourself.

Puberty is not just a series of changes but a process of becoming. It's about growing into the person you're meant to be, equipped with knowledge, strength, and the courage to face the world as your authentic self.

Embrace the changes with curiosity and confidence, knowing that every experience, challenge, and triumph is a step towards discovering your true self. Celebrate your growth, lean on your support system, and never be afraid to ask for help when needed.

Your teenage years are a time of transformation, exploration, and self-discovery. With each step, you're not only navigating the path of growing up but also laying the foundation for the incredible person you're becoming.

CHAPTER SUMMARY

- Puberty is a significant developmental phase in your teenage years, involving various biological processes that lead to physical and hormonal changes. Everyone's experience of puberty is different.
- Physical transformations that occur during puberty include growth spurts, breast development, the appearance of body hair, skin changes, and changes in body shape and composition. These changes are all a normal part of growing up.
- Menstruation is when your body sheds the lining of the uterus when there's no pregnancy. While dealing with periods may seem daunting initially, it's a sign that your body can create life.

- Many different products are available to help you manage your period. Tracking your menstrual cycles can help you predict when your period will arrive and notice any changes in your cycle.
- Puberty can often feel like an emotional rollercoaster. You may experience mood swings, navigate new feelings and attractions, and view body image differently.
- If you're unsure about any changes you experience to your body or mind, don't be afraid to seek help from a trusted adult or healthcare professional.
- Embrace puberty with confidence and curiosity. Puberty is a passage to discovering and becoming your true self.

CHAPTER 4
SCHOOL AND ACADEMICS

Starting your school journey with specific goals can help you navigate the challenging world of education and ensure you get to where you want to be. Setting academic goals is more than just aiming for good grades; it's about knowing what you want to achieve and how it fits your personal development and future dreams.

Firstly, let's discuss setting SMART goals. These are goals that are specific, measurable, achievable, relevant, and time-bound (SMART). For example, instead of saying, "I want to do better in math," a SMART goal would be, "I aim to improve my math grade from a B to an A by the end of the semester through weekly practice sessions and seeking extra help when needed." This goal is:

- Specific (improving math grade),
- Measurable (from a B to an A),
- Achievable (with dedicated effort),
- Relevant (important for your academic growth), and
- Time-bound (by the end of the semester)

Reflect on your strengths and areas for improvement. Are there subjects you're naturally drawn to or ones that require a bit more effort? Understanding this can help you tailor your goals to play to your strengths and challenge yourself in areas where there's room for growth.

You can set both short-term and long-term goals. Short-term goals could be related to upcoming tests, projects or improving participation in class discussions. Long-term goals might include maintaining a certain GPA or grade, participating in extracurricular activities, or preparing for college entrance exams. These goals complement each other, with short-term achievements paving the way for long-term aspirations.

Goal setting is a personal and continuous process. Your goals should reflect your ambitions and can change as you grow and gain more insight into your interests and potential career paths. Adjusting your goals as you discover new passions or face unexpected challenges is okay. What's important is that you're moving forward, learning, and growing.

Achieving a goal is a significant milestone in your academic journey and deserves recognition. Celebrating these victories, no matter how small, can boost your confidence and motivate you to set new goals.

As you continue to navigate your academic endeavors, remember that setting goals is about more than just academic success; it's about shaping your future, one step at a time. With each goal you set and achieve, you're building a strong academic foundation and developing skills and qualities that will serve you well beyond the classroom.

TIME MANAGEMENT AND ORGANIZATION TIPS

After you've set your academic goals, it's time to dive into the nitty-gritty of achieving them. This means mastering the art of time management and organization—a skill set crucial for your school years and life in general. Let's break it down into manageable parts?

Firstly, understand that time management is more than squeezing as many tasks into your day as possible. It's about simplifying how you work, doing things faster, and reducing stress. It's also about setting aside time for the people, play, and rest you love.

Use a Planner That Works for You

Whether it's a detailed agenda, a bullet journal, or a digital app, find a planner you enjoy using. This will be your roadmap, helping you navigate through your daily, weekly, and monthly tasks. Start by jotting down your fixed commitments like school, extracurricular activities, and family time. Then, block out time for homework, study sessions, and project work. Don't forget to schedule downtime for relaxation and fun activities to keep you motivated and happy.

Prioritize Your Tasks

Not all tasks are created equal. Learn to prioritize your work based on urgency and importance. A simple method is to categorize tasks into four quadrants: urgent and important, important but not urgent, urgent but not important, and neither urgent nor important. This will help you focus on what needs your attention daily and avoid getting bogged down by less critical tasks.

Break It Down

Large projects can feel overwhelming, but breaking them into smaller, more manageable tasks can make them more approachable. Set mini-deadlines for these tasks to keep yourself on track and prevent last-minute panic.

Find Your Productive Times

Are you a morning person or a night owl? Identifying when you're most alert and focused can help you plan your study sessions more effectively. Use these peak periods for tasks that require more concentration, saving easier or more routine tasks for when you might be less productive.

Stay Organized

Keep your workspace tidy and your school materials organized. This means having a designated spot for your textbooks, notebooks, and supplies. The less time you spend searching for things, the more time you have for actual work. Plus, a clutter-free space can help reduce stress and boost your focus.

Learn to Say No

Time is a finite resource, and it's okay to guard it with caution. You don't have to say yes to every social event, extra project, or additional responsibility. It's important to balance your academic commitments with your personal life but remember; it's okay to prioritize your needs and say no when you're stretched too thin.

Reflect and Adjust

Finally, take time to reflect on your time management and organizational strategies. What's working well? What could be improved? Adjust your methods to find what best suits your evolving schedule and priorities.

By mastering time management and organization, you're not just setting yourself up for academic success but building a foundation for a balanced, fulfilling life. It's about making the most of your time so you have more to spend on the things that truly matter to you.

ELLA BRADLEY

DEALING WITH ACADEMIC PRESSURE

In the stresses of school, where every grade feels like it could make or break your future, academic pressure can sometimes feel like an insurmountable mountain. But it's important to remember that mountains are climbed one step at a time. Let's talk about how to navigate the pressures of school without losing your joy and curiosity for learning.

Firstly, understand that it's completely normal to feel stressed about school. These feelings are valid, whether it's the fear of not living up to expectations or the overwhelming pile of assignments. However, they don't have to define your high school experience. One of the most empowering things you can do is recognize when you're feeling pressured and acknowledge these feelings without judgment. This self-awareness is your first step towards managing stress.

Next, let's talk about strategy. One practical approach is to break down your tasks into smaller, more manageable pieces. When faced with a daunting project or a study session for a big test, ask yourself, "What's one thing I can accomplish right now?" By focusing on one small task at a time, you can make steady progress without feeling overwhelmed.

Another key aspect of dealing with academic pressure is to set realistic goals. It's great to aim high, but setting goals that are too ambitious can lead to disappointment and increased stress. Instead, set achievable targets and celebrate your successes, no matter how small. This boosts your confidence and helps you maintain a positive outlook on your academic journey.

Feel free to reach out to teachers or counselors if you're struggling. They're there to support you, and often, they can offer perspectives or resources that can make a big difference. Sharing your feelings with friends or family can also lighten your emotional load. Many of your peers are likely experiencing similar pressures.

Lastly, it's essential to find balance. While academics are important, they're just one part of your life. Make time for activities that bring you joy and relaxation, whether pursuing a hobby, spending time with friends, or simply taking a moment to breathe and be present. These breaks are not a diversion from your goals but a vital component of a healthy, balanced life.

Academic pressure doesn't have to overshadow your school experience. You can navigate these challenges with grace and resilience by breaking tasks into manageable pieces, setting realistic goals, communicating openly, and finding balance. And remember, your grades do not define your worth. You are so much more. Let's carry this mindset as we explore the exciting world of extracurriculars, where you can further discover your passions and talents outside the classroom.

EXPLORING EXTRACURRICULARS

After navigating the waves of academic pressure, it's time to dive into the vibrant world of extracurricular activities. Think of this as your playground for growth, exploration, and fun outside your classrooms and textbooks. Extracurriculars are not just a break from academics; they're a crucial part of your teenage years, offering a unique blend of learning and enjoyment.

Extracurricular activities come in all shapes and sizes. From sports teams, music bands, and drama clubs to science fairs, debate teams, and student government, a world of options exists. Each one offers a unique opportunity to develop new skills, explore interests, and meet people with similar passions. The key is to find what excites you, what challenges you, and what makes you want to dive deeper.

But how do you choose with so many options available? Start by thinking about your interests and any skills you'd like to develop. Are you looking to express yourself creatively, or are you more intrigued by leadership opportunities? You may be passionate about social issues and want to make a difference. Once you have a clearer idea of your interests, research what your school and community offer. Don't be afraid to try something new or out of your comfort zone; you might discover a hidden talent or passion.

While it's tempting to sign up for every club and team that catches your eye, overcommitting can lead to burnout and stress, counteracting the benefits of these activities. It's all about balance. Aim for a mix that allows you to explore your interests without overwhelming your schedule. It's okay to start with one or two activities and adjust as you find your rhythm.

Participation in extracurriculars is also about building a supportive community. These activities provide a platform to form friendships and connections with peers who share your interests. It's a space where you can be yourself, learn from others, and grow together. Embrace the camaraderie and the shared experiences, whether celebrating a win, learning from a loss, or simply enjoying the process.

These activities equip you with valuable life skills. Leadership, teamwork, time management, and communication are just a few of the skills you'll develop. These abilities are not only beneficial for your personal growth but are also highly valued in college applications and future careers. Your involvement and achievements in extracurricular activities can shine on your resume, showcasing your initiative, interests, and dedication.

Enjoy exploring the world of extracurriculars. This is your time to shine in ways that academics alone might not allow. It's about discovering who you are, what you love, and how you can contribute to your community. Let your curiosity guide you, and don't be afraid to step out of your comfort zone. The experiences you gain here are invaluable, shaping you into a well-rounded woman ready to face the future confidently and enthusiastically.

The skills and passions you develop through extracurricular activities are building blocks for your future. They help you form a foundation for setting goals, planning, and dreaming big. Your journey through school is not just about grades; it's about becoming the best version of yourself, both inside and outside the classroom.

PLANNING FOR THE FUTURE

After diving into the world of extracurriculars, it's time to shift our focus toward a broader horizon—planning for the future. This is not just about choosing the right college or career path; it's about understanding yourself, your passions, and how they translate into a fulfilling future.

Firstly, let's talk about setting goals. Goals guide you where you want to go, and it's okay if these goals evolve. Start by asking yourself what you enjoy doing, what subjects you excel in, and how you see yourself making a difference in the world. These questions don't need immediate answers but are important to consider as you plan.

Next, research is your best friend. Whether you dream of becoming a software engineer, a graphic designer, or a marine biologist, there's a wealth of information out there. Consider what courses you should take in high school to prepare for your chosen field. Explore universities and colleges, considering their academic offerings, culture, location, and extracurricular opportunities. Websites, college fairs, and informational interviews are fantastic resources to help you gather insights.

Speaking of preparation, standardized tests like the SAT or ACT are often critical components of college applications. While they're not the only factor in admissions decisions, doing well can certainly boost your prospects. Consider starting your test prep early, identifying areas where you need improvement, and seeking resources, be it books, online courses, or tutoring, to help you succeed.

Financial planning is another crucial aspect. College can be expensive, but don't let that discourage you. Start exploring scholarships, grants, and work-study programs early on. Many organizations offer scholarships based on merit, community service, or specific career interests. Your school's guidance counselor can be a great resource in finding opportunities that align with your goals.

Planning for the future is not just about academics and career paths. It's also about developing life skills that will serve you well regardless of where you end up. Time management, communication, and critical thinking are just as important as your GPA. So, while working hard in school, don't forget to invest time growing these essential skills.

As you start the exciting process of planning for the future, stay true to yourself. Your future is not just about what you do; it's about who you become in the process. Embrace the process, and know that every step you take is a step toward a future that's uniquely yours.

CHAPTER SUMMARY

- Setting academic goals is crucial for guiding your path through school, focusing on SMART goals for personal growth and future aspirations.
- Reflect on your strengths and areas for improvement to tailor goals that challenge you and play to your strengths, setting both short-term and long-term objectives.
- Goal setting is a personal and dynamic process, allowing for adjustments as you grow and discover new interests, with achievements deserving celebration.
- Mastering time management and organization is essential for academic success, involving creating a planner, prioritizing tasks, and finding productive times.
- Dealing with academic pressure involves recognizing stress, breaking tasks into manageable pieces, setting realistic goals, and finding a balance between academics and personal life.
- Exploring extracurricular activities offers opportunities for growth, exploration, and fun, helping to develop new skills and build a supportive community.
- Participation in extracurriculars also equips you with valuable life skills like leadership and teamwork, which can benefit college applications and future careers.
- Planning for the future involves setting goals, researching career paths, preparing for standardized tests, financial planning, and developing essential life skills, all while staying true to yourself.

CHAPTER 5
YOUR DIGITAL WORLD

The digital world is where friendships can blossom, ideas can be shared, and voices can be heard. Navigating this space requires wisdom, courage, and a dash of savvy. Let's explore how to make the most of your social media experience while safeguarding your well-being.

Your online presence is an extension of you. Just as you choose outfits that reflect your style or speak words that echo your thoughts, your social media profiles should mirror the authentic you. But with authenticity comes responsibility. Before you post, pause and ponder: Is this something I'd be comfortable with everyone seeing? This includes your family, future employers, or even a college admissions officer. The internet holds onto our digital footprints indefinitely.

Engagement on social media is like a conversation at a bustling party. You'll encounter different opinions, personalities, and sometimes, unwelcome comments. While standing up for your beliefs is essential, choosing your battles wisely is key. Not every comment needs a response, and not every post deserves your energy. Navigating these interactions with a discerning eye and resilient mindset will protect your mental health and enrich your online experience.

Comparison, the thief of happiness, thrives on social media. It's easy to fall into the trap of comparing your reality with everyone else's online profile. But remember, what people choose to share online is just a fraction of their reality. Celebrate your achievements, big or small, and use the success of others as inspiration, not as the basis for your self-worth.

Privacy settings are your digital armor. Regularly reviewing who has access to your personal information and posts is crucial. Set your social media accounts to private so you have control over who can see your posts. Social media platforms often update their privacy policies and settings, so staying informed will help you maintain control over your online space. Share with intention, knowing that once something is out in the digital universe, it's out of your hands.

Lastly, try a digital detox. Just as your body needs rest from physical activities, your mind benefits from breaks from social media. Designate times to unplug and reconnect with the world beyond the screen. Whether reading a book, spending time in nature or practicing a hobby, these moments of disconnection will recharge your spirit and enhance your real-life connections.

By approaching social media with intention, empathy, and awareness, you'll protect your digital footprint and cultivate a space that reflects the best of you.

HOW TO BE SAFE ONLINE

Your safety is paramount in the vast expanse of the digital world. As you've learned to navigate the complexities of social media online, it's equally important to understand how to protect yourself in the digital world. While a treasure trove of information and connectivity, the internet can also be full of risks if not approached with caution and knowledge.

First and foremost, remember that not everything or everyone online is as they appear. The anonymity of the internet allows people to present themselves in any way they choose, which isn't always truthful. Be skeptical of strangers contacting you online, especially if they request personal information or suggest meeting in person. Trust your instincts—if something feels off, it probably is.

Creating strong, unique passwords for your online accounts is a simple yet effective step to help protect your digital presence. Avoid using easily guessable information like your birthdate or pet's name, because these are the first things someone will try if they attempt to hack your account. Instead, opt for a mix of letters, numbers, and symbols, and consider using a password manager to keep track of them all. Regularly updating your passwords can also add an extra layer of security.

Be mindful of the information you share on social media and other online platforms. Once something is posted online, it can be difficult, if not impossible, to completely erase. Think twice before sharing personal details that could be used to identify or locate you, such as your home address, phone number, or school. Adjust your privacy settings to control who can see your posts and personal information. Be cautious about accepting friend requests from people you don't know in real life.

Cyberbullying is another harsh reality of the online world. If you find yourself targeted, know it's not your fault, and you're not alone. Reach out to a trusted adult—a parent, teacher, or counselor—for support. Most social media platforms have tools that allow you to report harassment and block users who are being abusive.

Lastly, be aware of phishing attempts and scams. These can come in emails, messages, or even advertisements that trick you into giving away personal information or downloading malicious software. Always verify the source before clicking on links or providing any data.

It's also essential to consider how we interact with the digital world and how it affects us. The time we spend staring at screens and consuming content can significantly impact our mental and physical health. By staying informed and making conscious choices, we can enjoy the benefits of the internet while minimizing its risks.

THE IMPACT OF SCREEN TIME

As technology becomes a bigger part of our everyday lives, it's easy to overlook the silent shadow that follows us everywhere:

screen time. Amidst the endless streams of social media, online homework, and video chats, it's crucial to pause and reflect on how our digital habits shape our well-being, relationships, and perception of the world.

Firstly, let's talk about the elephant in the room - how much is too much? While there's no one-size-fits-all answer, it's important to recognize when screen time starts to interfere with our sleep, physical activity, and face-to-face interactions. Have you ever found yourself scrolling through your phone late at night, only to realize it's way past your bedtime? Or perhaps you've missed a family gathering because you were too engrossed in a video game. These moments are signals, gentle nudges reminding us to reassess and recalibrate our digital consumption.

The impact of excessive screen time isn't just about missing out on real-life experiences; it also affects our mental health. Studies have shown a link between prolonged screen time and increased feelings of anxiety and depression. It's like being caught in a loop - we turn to our screens for a quick dopamine hit, a momentary escape from our worries, only to find ourselves feeling more isolated and stressed than before. The key is finding balance and using technology as a tool that adds value to our lives rather than detracts from it.

So, how can we achieve this ultimate balance? It starts with self-awareness. Pay attention to how you feel during and after screen time. Are you energized and inspired, or do you feel drained and disheartened? Listen to your body and mind; they often give us the cues to adjust our habits. Setting boundaries is also crucial. Designate tech-free zones and times in your day, especially before bedtime, to help your mind unwind and prepare for restful sleep.

It's not about hating technology or cutting it out of our lives entirely. After all, the online world offers incredible opportunities for learning, creativity, and connection. It's about fostering a relationship with technology that supports our well-being, respects our time, and enhances our real-world experiences.

Our digital footprints are not just the traces we leave online, but also the imprint technology leaves on us. By navigating our digital world with intention and mindfulness, we can use the power of technology to build a brighter, more connected future.

YOUR DIGITAL FOOTPRINT AND PRIVACY

In a world where your digital presence can be as significant as your physical one, understanding your digital footprint and how to protect your privacy becomes essential. Whenever you post a photo, comment on social media, or even search for something online, you add to your digital footprint. It's like leaving little digital breadcrumbs everywhere you go on the internet. These breadcrumbs can tell a story about who you are, what you like, and even where you live. While it's fun to share parts of your life online, knowing how these pieces of information can be seen, used, and even misused is essential.

First, let's talk about what a digital footprint is. Imagine every action you take online leaves a mark, just like footprints in the sand. Only these footprints don't wash away with the tide; they stay there, accumulating over time. This includes the obvious stuff, like your social media profiles and the photos you share, but also the things you might not think about, like the location data on your phone or your search engine history.

Now, why should you care? Your digital footprint can affect your future in ways you might not expect. College admissions officers, potential employers, and even future partners might look you up online to see what kind of person you are. What they find can influence their decisions about you. Plus, there's the issue of privacy. The more information about you that's out there, the easier it is for someone to misuse it, whether that's stealing your identity or harassing you online.

So, how can you protect your digital footprint and your privacy? Here are some practical tips:

- **Think Before You Share**: Before posting anything online, ask yourself if it's something you'd be comfortable with everyone seeing, including your future self. It's hard to take back once it's out there.
- **Check Your Privacy Settings**: Social media platforms often update their privacy settings. Make it a habit to check yours regularly to ensure you only share information with people you trust.
- **Be Password Wise**: Use strong, unique passwords for different accounts. Consider using a password manager to keep track of them. This helps protect your accounts from being hacked.
- **Google Yourself**: It might sound funny, but searching for yourself online can show you what others see when they look you up. If you find information you're uncomfortable with, look into how to remove it.
- **Educate Yourself**: Stay informed about the latest in internet safety and privacy. The more you know, the better you can protect yourself.

Your digital world is an extension of your real one. By managing your digital footprint and protecting your privacy, you're safeguarding your information and shaping how the world sees you. As we embrace technology for the incredible tool it is, let's do so with awareness and care, ensuring that our digital selves reflect our true values and aspirations.

HOW TO USE TECHNOLOGY FOR GOOD

In the digital age, where every click, like, and share shapes the world around us, it's empowering to know that technology isn't just a tool for communication—it's a platform for change. As you navigate your digital world, know that your online presence is also a canvas for painting your impact on the world. Here are some ways to use technology for good, transforming digital interactions into positive actions that ripple through the online and offline world.

- **Empower and Educate Yourself**: The internet is a treasure trove of knowledge. Use it to learn about causes you care about, whether climate change, social justice, or mental health awareness. Knowledge is power; the more informed you are, the better equipped you'll be to make a difference.
- **Spread Positivity**: Social media can sometimes feel like a battleground but can also be a place of support and positivity. Share uplifting stories, positive news, and words of encouragement. A simple, kind message can brighten someone's day and potentially change a life.
- **Advocate for Causes**: Use your digital voice to support causes close to your heart. Sign online petitions, join virtual protests, and support non-profit organizations through social media campaigns. Your voice matters;

when combined with millions of others online, it can lead to real-world change.
- **Volunteer Virtually**: Many organizations offer virtual volunteering opportunities. This can include tutoring students online, providing emotional support through digital platforms, or assisting with remote research projects. These experiences can help you give back to the community and help you form new connections.
- **Be a Responsible Digital Citizen**: Be mindful of the content you share and promote. Check information before spreading it, and always aim to contribute positively to online discussions.
- **Create and Share**: You have the power to create content that matters. Start a blog, a podcast, or a video channel focused on topics that inspire change. Use your creativity to shed light on important issues, share stories that matter, and inspire others to join your cause.

In embracing these practices, you're actively shaping the digital landscape into a force for good. Each positive action, no matter how small, contributes to a larger wave of change. Understand the power of your online presence as you continue to explore your digital world. Use it wisely, use it kindly, and most importantly, use it for good.

CHAPTER SUMMARY

- Social media is a powerful tool for connection and expression, but it requires careful navigation to protect your mental health and well-being.

- Authenticity online is crucial, and you must consider the long-term visibility of the content you share and its potential impact.
- Engaging wisely on social media involves choosing your battles and protecting mental health when faced with diverse opinions and negativity.
- Comparison on social media can affect your self-worth; privacy settings serve as a digital safeguard.
- Regular digital detoxes are beneficial for mental health and enhancing real-life connections.
- Online safety is paramount. You should be skeptical towards strangers, use strong passwords, and be cautious about sharing your personal information online.
- The impact of too much screen time includes disrupted sleep and increased anxiety, highlighting the need for balanced digital habits.
- Using technology for good involves educating yourself, spreading positivity, advocating for causes, virtual volunteering, and responsible digital citizenship.

CHAPTER 6
UNDERSTANDING RELATIONSHIPS

Navigating family dynamics can often feel like trying to solve a puzzle with pieces that don't quite fit. Each family is unique, with its own set of values, traditions, and ways of communicating. Understanding and finding your place within this dynamic can be both challenging and enriching.

Family relationships are fundamental to how we view the world and ourselves. These relationships can influence our self-esteem, choices, and future relationships. It is no surprise that fostering healthy family dynamics is pivotal to our well-being. This doesn't mean your family needs to be perfect. Still, it's about striving for a balance where you can communicate openly and respect each other.

Communication is the foundation of any relationship, and it's no different within the family. Encourage open dialogues with your family members. Share your thoughts, feelings, and experiences with them, and equally, listen to theirs. It's okay to agree to disagree on certain topics. What's important is that everyone feels heard and respected.

Respect is another crucial element. Respect goes beyond basic manners; it's about acknowledging each other's individuality, boundaries, and personal space. As you grow and evolve, so too will your views and opinions. Respecting these changes in each other can strengthen your family bonds.

Boundaries are equally important in family dynamics. Setting healthy boundaries with family members helps you establish your identity and independence. It's about finding the balance between being connected to your family and having the space to explore who you are.

Conflict is inevitable in any relationship, and families are no exception. When conflicts arise, approach them as opportunities for growth. Try to resolve conflicts through open communication, empathy, and understanding. It's not about winning an argument but finding a solution that respects everyone's feelings and needs.

Lastly, spend quality time together. In today's fast-paced world, it's easy to get caught up in our lives and forget to connect with family members. Make an effort to engage in activities that bring you closer, whether it's a family game night, cooking a meal together, or simply talking over dinner.

Understanding and navigating family dynamics requires patience, empathy, and love. By fostering open communication, respect, healthy boundaries, and spending quality time together, you can build a strong foundation that supports you as you explore the broader world of relationships outside your family circle.

HEALTHY ROMANTIC RELATIONSHIPS

Navigating romantic relationships can be both thrilling and daunting. As you step into this new realm, it's crucial to understand what a healthy romantic relationship looks like. This understanding will empower you to make informed decisions that respect your well-being and that of your partner.

Communication is one of the most essential components of any healthy relationship. It's more than just sharing your thoughts and feelings; it's also about listening and truly hearing what your partner says. Effective communication involves expressing yourself openly and honestly, without fear of judgment, and being receptive to your partner's perspective. It's okay to agree to disagree on some things. What's important is how you handle these differences, approaching them with respect and empathy.

Trust and respect are two sides of the same coin in a healthy romantic relationship. Trust builds over time and can help you feel secure with your partner. It means knowing that you can rely on each other no matter what arises. On the other hand, respect involves acknowledging each other's individuality and valuing each other's opinions and boundaries. It's about treating each other with kindness and consideration, even when you disagree.

Speaking of boundaries, they are essential in any relationship. Boundaries help define what you are comfortable with and how you wish to be treated by your partner. They can be about anything - your time, energy, body, or possessions. Establishing and respecting boundaries is a sign of mutual respect and understanding. It's okay to say no, and listening when your partner says it is important, too.

Equality is another key aspect of a healthy romantic relationship. This means sharing power and making decisions together rather than one person calling all the shots. It's about giving and taking in equal measure, ensuring both partners feel valued and heard. Whether it's about choosing a movie to watch or making plans for the future, both partners should have an equal say.

Lastly, support is what binds all these elements together. Supporting each other through thick and thin, celebrating each other's successes, and being there during tough times make a relationship strong. It's about being each other's cheerleader, offering encouragement, and believing in each other's dreams and abilities.

If you find yourself in a relationship lacking these healthy qualities or realize some values are missing, take a step back and assess your situation. Reflect on what aspects of the relationship are causing discomfort or unhappiness.

In these situations, communication, as always, is vital. Try to have an open and honest conversation with your partner about your concerns, expressing your feelings without placing blame. Through dialogue, both of you can work towards improving the relationship. However, if attempts at communication don't lead to positive changes, or if the relationship is causing you more harm than good, it might be necessary to consider letting go.

Prioritizing your mental and emotional well-being is not selfish—it's necessary. Seeking support from friends, family, or a professional can give you the guidance and perspective needed during such times. Ending a relationship, especially one that's unhealthy, can be difficult, but it's a step towards finding happiness and fulfillment on your own terms. Being in a healthy relationship means being in a space where you feel valued, respected, and free to be yourself. If you don't feel that way in a relationship, think about why, and consider if it's right for you.

As you form new romantic relationships, remember that it's a learning process. There will be ups and downs, but each experience offers valuable lessons. Stay true to yourself, communicate openly, and treat your partner with kindness and respect. By doing so, you'll not only foster a healthy romantic relationship but also grow as a person. And remember that you don't have to be in a romantic relationship to live your best life. You don't need anyone else to complete you - you are already complete.

HOW TO SET BOUNDARIES

When it comes to understanding relationships, setting boundaries is an essential step that often gets overlooked. It's like drawing a personal map that outlines where you are comfortable and where you start to feel uneasy. Boundaries are not about building walls around you but about drawing lines that help others understand how to treat you respectfully and lovingly.

Imagine you're painting a masterpiece that is your life. You wouldn't want someone else grabbing the brush and deciding your colors, right? Similarly, setting boundaries is about taking control of your own brush, choosing your colors, and deciding how close someone can get to your canvas. It's saying, "This is okay with me, and this is not."

But how do you start setting these boundaries? It begins with self-awareness. Understand what makes you feel comfortable, respected, and happy in a relationship. Are there certain behaviors or situations that make you feel uncomfortable or disrespected? Recognizing these feelings is the first step.

Next, communicate your boundaries clearly and assertively. It's not about being confrontational but about being honest and direct. For instance, if you need time to yourself, you might say, "I value our time together, but I also need some time alone to recharge. Can we plan some time apart this weekend?" This way, you express your needs while showing that you value the relationship.

It's okay for your boundaries to evolve as you grow and learn more about yourself. What's important is that you're making choices that honor your well-being and respect.

Setting boundaries might feel awkward initially, especially if you're not used to putting yourself first and asserting your needs. But with practice, it becomes easier. And the right people will respect your boundaries and appreciate honest communication. They'll understand that respecting your boundaries can make the relationship stronger and more meaningful.

In the grand scheme of things, setting boundaries is not just about protecting yourself; it's about creating healthy, respectful, and loving relationships. It teaches others how to treat you and, importantly, how to respect and prioritize your needs and feelings.

As you continue to build and let go of relationships in your teens, remember that experiencing heartbreak is a part of the journey. It shows our ability to love and connect deeply with others. While it may seem disheartening, navigating these emotions is crucial for personal growth and building future relationships.

HOW TO DEAL WITH HEARTBREAK

Heartbreak, while one of the most challenging experiences you may experience, is also a profound teacher. Heartbreak is a universal feeling, but when it happens to you, it can feel like you're the only one in the world who has ever felt this way. The pain is real, and it's okay to acknowledge it. Let's have a look at how to navigate this experience together so you can learn how to heal and grow from it.

First, allow yourself to feel. It's okay to cry, be angry, or feel numb. These emotions are all part of the healing process. Trying to push these feelings away can prolong the pain. Instead, find a safe space where you can express your emotions freely. This could be through writing in a journal, talking to a trusted friend or family member, or even creating art. Expression is a powerful tool for healing.

Healing is not linear. Some days will be better than others. You might feel like you're taking two steps forward and one step back, but this is normal. Be patient with yourself and recognize that healing takes time. There's no set timeline for when you should "be over it." Everyone's experience is unique.

It's important to surround yourself with a supportive community during this time. Lean on friends and family who understand and respect your need to heal. Sometimes, well-meaning people might say things like "There are plenty of fish in the sea" or "You'll get over it soon." While they're trying to help, these phrases might not be what you need to hear right now. It's okay to communicate your needs and set boundaries around the support you're looking for.

Do things that bring you happiness and fulfillment. It might be hard to feel motivated, but participating in hobbies or interests you love can help lift your spirits. Whether it's painting, playing some music, or spending time in nature, these activities can offer a sense of normalcy and joy during this time and help you realize that this isn't the be-all and end-all.

Lastly, once you feel ready, reflect on what you've learned from the relationship. No matter how it ends, every relationship teaches us something about ourselves and what we want in future relationships. Take time to understand what you valued in the relationship and what you might do differently next time. This reflection is not about assigning blame but growing and understanding yourself better. You could write this in a journal or talk to a friend about it.

Dealing with heartbreak is a deeply personal journey and an opportunity for you to grow as a person. By allowing yourself to feel, seeking support, and reflecting on your experiences, you're laying the groundwork for healing and moving forward. It's not just about getting over someone but about becoming a stronger, more resilient version of yourself.

THE IMPORTANCE OF SELF-LOVE

One of the most profound discoveries you'll make in understanding relationships is the importance of self-love. It's a concept that might seem obvious at first, but its depth and significance are often overlooked. After navigating the challenging waters of heartbreak, it becomes even more important to anchor yourself in the practice of self-love.

Self-love isn't just about pampering yourself with a spa day or treating yourself to your favorite dessert—though those moments are enjoyable and absolutely encouraged. It's about cultivating a deep, unwavering respect and appreciation for yourself and your needs and boundaries.

Self-love is integral to healthy relationships. It teaches you to value yourself and recognize your worth independently of anyone else's validation. This is essential because when you understand your value, you're less likely to settle for relationships that aren't good for you. You become better at recognizing red flags and more empowered to walk away from situations that don't serve your best interests.

But how do you cultivate self-love, especially in the aftermath of heartbreak? It starts with self-compassion. Be gentle with yourself. Understand that you don't have to heal immediately and that it's okay to have days when you feel less than your best. Embrace your imperfections and learn from your mistakes rather than criticizing yourself. Everyone faces challenges and setbacks; what matters most is how you rise from them.

Next, invest time in understanding yourself. Explore your interests, passions, and values. What makes you feel alive? What are your dreams and aspirations? The more you know about yourself, the more you'll love yourself. This self-knowledge also acts as a compass, guiding you towards relationships that align with your true self.

Setting boundaries is another crucial aspect of self-love. Learn to say no to things that drain your energy or go against your values. This might be challenging, especially if you're used to putting others' needs before your own. However, setting boundaries is a powerful way to honor yourself. It communicates to others that you respect yourself and sets the tone for how you expect to be treated.

Finally, surround yourself with positivity. Look for friends and mentors who uplift you, see your potential, and encourage you to pursue your dreams. The people you spend time with significantly impact how you see yourself and the world around you. Choose wisely.

In essence, self-love is about treating yourself with the same kindness, respect, and care you would offer to someone you deeply love. It's a journey, not a destination, and it's one of the most rewarding journeys you'll ever embark on. As you grow in self-love, you'll find that your relationships become more fulfilling, not because they define you but because they complement the love you've already cultivated within yourself.

CHAPTER SUMMARY

- Understanding family dynamics involves open communication, respect, and setting healthy boundaries to foster a balanced relationship.
- Encouraging open dialogues, respecting individuality, and managing conflicts through empathy are key to strengthening family bonds.
- Spending quality time with family is essential to maintain close relationships in today's fast-paced world.
- Effective communication, trust, respect, and equality are foundational elements for a healthy partnership in romantic relationships.
- Setting boundaries in relationships is about asserting your needs and comfort levels, which is crucial for personal well-being and respect.
- Dealing with heartbreak involves allowing yourself to feel emotions, seeking support, and engaging in

- fulfilling activities, emphasizing it as an opportunity for personal growth.
- Cultivating self-love is fundamental in the aftermath of heartbreak, focusing on self-compassion, understanding personal values, and setting boundaries.
- Self-love is the foundation for healthy relationships, teaching the importance of valuing yourself and fostering relationships that honor your worth.

CHAPTER 7
FACING CHALLENGES

F ailure is a word that carries a lot of weight, especially during your teenage years. But here's the thing about failure: it's not the end of your story. Failure is a vital part of your growth. Overcoming failure is learning how to stand up after a fall, dust yourself off, and keep moving forward with resilience and grace.

First and foremost, understand that failure is universal. Every person you admire, every role model or hero, has faced their failures. What sets them apart is not their invincibility but their ability to keep going despite setbacks. So, when you face failure, remember you're in good company.

One practical step to overcoming failure is to reframe how you view it. Instead of seeing failure as a negative thing, view it as an opportunity to learn. Ask yourself, "What can this experience teach me?" This shift in perspective can transform failure from a stumbling block to a stepping stone.

Another strategy is to practice self-compassion. Be kind to yourself in moments of failure. Speak to yourself as you would to a close friend facing the same situation. This kindness doesn't mean making excuses for your mistakes but acknowledging your humanity and permitting yourself to try again.

Setting small, achievable goals can also help you regain confidence. After a setback, tackling big projects or goals can feel intimidating. Break your larger goals into smaller, manageable tasks. Celebrate each small milestone along the way. This process helps rebuild your self-esteem and momentum.

Don't be afraid to reach out to others. Sharing your disappointment or frustration with trusted friends, family members, or mentors can give you a fresh perspective and much-needed encouragement. Sometimes, knowing you're not alone in your struggles can make all the difference.

Overcoming failure is not about never falling; it's about learning how to rise every time you do. It's about building resilience, embracing growth, and understanding that each setback is a part of your journey toward becoming the best version of yourself.

Another challenge that often arises during our lives is dealing with bullying. While difficult, this issue can be overcome with the right tools and support. You can stand firm against bullying and advocate for a kinder, more inclusive environment for yourself and others.

HOW TO DEAL WITH BULLYING

Bullying is a challenge that many face, but it's one you can navigate through with strength and courage. There are numerous strategies you can use to protect yourself and seek support.

Firstly, recognize that bullying is never your fault. Bullies often target others due to their insecurities or issues. Understanding this doesn't excuse their behavior but can help you see that their actions reflect on them, not you.

One practical step you can take is to document instances of bullying. Keep a record of what happened, when, and where. This can be useful if you must report the behavior to someone in authority, like a teacher or school counselor.

Speaking of which, don't be afraid to reach out for help. It might feel scary and confronting, but there are people who care about you and want to support you. Whether it's a trusted adult, a close friend, or a professional, sharing your experience can lighten your burden and open pathways for resolving the situation.

Another key strategy is to build a support network. Surround yourself with positive influences—friends who uplift you, family members who listen, and activities that bring you joy. These positive connections can bolster your self-esteem and remind you of your worth, especially when bullies try to tear you down.

In the digital age, bullying can also take place online. It's crucial to practice safe online habits: keep personal information private, think before you post, and don't be afraid to block or report someone who is being hurtful. The anonymity of the internet can strengthen bullies, so protecting your digital footprint is more important than ever.

Work on building your resilience. This doesn't mean you have to deal with bullying alone or pretend that it doesn't affect you. Instead, it's about developing coping strategies that help you bounce back. Whether through creative outlets like writing and art, physical activity, or mindfulness practices like meditation, find what helps you maintain your equilibrium and sense of calm.

Facing bullying is about more than just getting through it. It's about growing through it, learning about your strengths, and understanding that your value is not determined by anyone else's words or actions. As you navigate these challenges of teenage life, you're not just surviving; you're learning, growing, and becoming even stronger. And that's something truly powerful.

NAVIGATING MENTAL HEALTH ISSUES

As we explored in earlier chapters, mental health is crucial to your overall well-being. Just like physical health, it needs attention, care, and, sometimes, professional intervention. It's okay to feel lost sometimes, not to have all the answers, or to realize that your path might need a change of direction. It's normal to experience a range of emotions. Still, when these feelings interfere with your day-to-day life, it's essential to take action.

One of the most empowering steps you can take is to educate yourself about mental health. Knowledge truly is power. Understanding the signs and symptoms of common mental health issues can help you recognize them in yourself or others. This awareness can be the first step towards seeking help or offering support.

Reaching out for help is a sign of strength, not weakness. Whether it's talking to a trusted adult, a friend, or a mental health professional, sharing your feelings and experiences can be incredibly relieving and is an integral part of managing mental health issues. Remember that there are people who want to help you navigate these challenges so you don't have to go through them alone.

Self-care is another vital aspect of managing mental health. Self-care can look different for everyone. For some, it might be engaging in a favorite hobby. For others, it might be practicing mindfulness or exercise. The key is to find activities that bring you joy and relaxation and make them a regular part of your routine.

Mental health issues don't define you or your worth. They are just one part of the complex, beautiful person that you are. Embracing and working through your vulnerabilities can help you become more self-aware and empowered.

Life is a series of ups and downs. Loss, in its many forms, is an inevitable part of life. Learning to cope with loss is not just about finding ways to move on but also about allowing yourself to feel, to grieve, and to eventually find a way to heal.

HOW TO COPE WITH LOSS

Coping with loss is an experience that touches everyone at some point. During your teenage years, it can feel particularly overwhelming. Loss comes in many forms: the death of a loved one, the end of a friendship, or even the loss of something intangible, like a sense of security following a traumatic event. It's a challenge that can feel overwhelming, but with the right tools, you can navigate grief no matter what life throws you.

Grief doesn't have a one-size-fits-all solution and doesn't adhere to a strict timeline. You might feel a whirlwind of emotions: sadness, anger, confusion, or even relief, and these feelings might change from day to day. That's perfectly normal. Allow yourself to feel whatever comes up for you without judgment.

One of the most practical steps you can take is to express your feelings. This could be through talking with someone you trust, like a friend, family member, or counselor. If verbal expression feels daunting, consider writing in a journal, creating art, or engaging in another form of self-expression. Sometimes, putting your feelings into words or actions can help to process them.

Seeking support is crucial. Surround yourself with people who understand and respect your need to grieve. Support groups, either in-person or online, can also be valuable. Connecting with others who have experienced similar losses can provide comfort and understanding you might not find elsewhere.

Remember to take care of your physical self as well. Grief can be exhausting, both emotionally and physically. Try to maintain a routine that includes regular meals, some form of physical activity, and plenty of rest. It's okay if you're not operating at 100%—what's important is that you're taking steps to care for your well-being.

Lastly, be patient with yourself. Healing from loss is a journey, not a destination. There will be good days and bad days. Over time, the intensity of your grief will change, and you might find yourself discovering new ways to cope that you hadn't considered before. This process is part of finding your strength and perseverance, ready to be uncovered.

Coping with loss is not about forgetting or moving on from the person or thing you've lost. It's about finding a way to carry that loss with you in a way that honors your experience and its impact on your life. You can navigate this path, equipped with the tools to face the challenge, and ultimately, find a way to weave this experience into your identity.

FINDING RESILIENCE

After navigating the stormy seas of loss, it's time to anchor ourselves in the harbor of resilience. Resilience isn't just about bouncing back; it's about growing through what you go through. It's about finding that inner strength that helps you face life's challenges head-on, even when you feel like you're walking against a hurricane.

Resilience is not a natural trait that only a few possess. It's a skill; like all skills, it can be developed with practice and patience. Think of it as a muscle that gets stronger each time you use it. Every challenge you face and overcome is like a workout for your resilience muscle.

One way to build resilience is by maintaining a positive outlook. This doesn't mean ignoring your problems or pretending everything is fine when it's not. It means acknowledging your situation and believing in your ability to get through it. It's about focusing on what you can control and letting go of what you can't. Optimism is a choice, and it's a powerful one.

Another aspect of finding resilience is to lean on your support system. Whether it's family, friends, or a mentor, having people you can turn to for encouragement and advice can make all the difference. These people will remind you of your strength when you forget and will stand by you through thick and thin. Reaching out is not a sign of weakness; it's a sign of wisdom.

Self-care is also crucial in building resilience. This means taking care of your body, mind, and spirit. Eat healthily, get enough sleep, exercise, and find time to do things that make you happy. When you're physically and emotionally well, you're in a better position to handle stress and bounce back from setbacks.

Finally, embrace failure as part of the learning process. Every mistake, every failure, is an opportunity to grow. Instead of beating yourself up, ask yourself, "What can I learn from this?" The most successful people are those who have failed the most. They're not defined by their failures but by how they've overcome them.

Building resilience is about continuously striving to be the best version of yourself, even when the going gets tough. So, when you face your next challenge, remember that you have the strength to overcome it.

CHAPTER SUMMARY

- Failure is a natural part of personal growth. It teaches us resilience and perseverance and should be viewed as a learning opportunity rather than a negative experience.
- Practicing self-compassion and setting small, achievable goals can help you rebuild confidence and momentum after a setback.
- Seeking support from friends, family, or mentors can provide encouragement and a fresh perspective on failure.
- Bullying, including digital bullying, could be addressed by documenting incidents, seeking help, and building a support network to boost your self-esteem.

- Mental health is vital to your overall well-being. It can require you to learn, reach out for help, practice self-care, and understand that it's okay not to be okay.
- Coping with loss involves acknowledging and expressing your feelings, seeking support, caring for your physical health, and being patient with the healing process.
- Resilience can be developed through maintaining a positive outlook, leaning on a support system, and viewing failure as a learning opportunity.
- The journey through life challenges like failure, bullying, mental health issues, and loss teaches us resilience, strength, and the importance of support and self-care.

CHAPTER 8
EXPRESSING YOURSELF

Discovering your passions through self-expression is like uncovering hidden treasures within yourself. It's about peeling back the layers to reveal what makes your heart sing, ignites that spark of excitement, and gives you a sense of purpose. This exploration is not just about identifying what you enjoy but understanding how these passions reflect your unique identity and how they can be a source of strength and empowerment.

Embarking on this quest requires curiosity and an open mind. Start by thinking about moments when you felt most alive or lost track of time because you were so engrossed in an activity. These moments are clues pointing toward your passions. It could be anything from the thrill of solving a hard math problem to the satisfaction of creating art or the joy of storytelling. Passions are not limited to talents; they are about what brings you joy and fulfillment.

Experimentation plays a crucial role in this discovery process. It's okay not to have all the answers right away. Allow yourself to try new things, whether joining a club, learning a new skill, or volunteering for a cause that interests you. Each experience is a step closer to understanding what excites you. Embrace the process with patience and an open heart, knowing your passions may evolve.

As you discover your passions, listen to your inner voice. In a world constantly buzzing with opinions and expectations, it's easy to be influenced by what others think you should be passionate about. Trust your instincts and follow what excites you, not what seems popular or approved by others. Your passions are uniquely yours; they reflect your inner world and are a source of your uniqueness.

Sharing your passions with others can be both exhilarating and intimidating. Fear of judgment or not being good enough can hold you back. However, expressing your passions is not about seeking approval but honoring your authentic self. It's about creating connections, inspiring others, and finding your tribe—people who share similar interests or appreciate your enthusiasm.

Passions add richness and excitement to your life. They are not just hobbies or interests but expressions of your deepest self, guiding lights that lead you toward contentment and happiness. As you continue to explore and embrace your passions, you'll find that they enrich your life and empower you to express your unique voice in this world.

Consider how these passions can be channeled into creative outlets. Creativity is not confined to the arts; it's a way of thinking, a means of expressing your individuality, and a tool for navigating the complexities of life. The following section will explore various creative outlets and how they can be powerful vehicles for self-expression and personal growth.

CREATIVE OUTLETS

Finding ways to express yourself is as vital as the air you breathe. It's about letting the world see a glimpse of your inner universe, thoughts, emotions, and perspectives. Creative outlets offer you a stage to channel your innermost feelings into something tangible that speaks when words fall short.

Creativity isn't confined to the arts alone, though painting, writing, and music are powerful mediums of expression. It's also found in how you solve problems, decorate your space, and even the joy of preparing a meal. The essence of creativity lies in creating something that reflects you.

If you're drawn to visual arts, consider keeping a sketchbook. It's a private space where you can experiment with colors, shapes, and textures without the pressure of an audience. If words are your chosen medium, a journal can be your companion. Write poems and stories, or pour out your thoughts and dreams. It's not about crafting a masterpiece; it's about the process and act of expressing what's within.

Music offers another way to connect with your emotions. Learning an instrument, singing, or creating playlists that reflect your mood can be incredibly therapeutic. It's a way to say things out loud without finding the exact words.

Technology has broadened the horizon for creative expression. Digital art, blogging, and video creation allow you to share your voice with a broader audience. These platforms enable you to express yourself and connect with others who share your passions and struggles.

The goal of exploring creative outlets isn't perfection. It's about finding joy in creating and learning more about yourself. It's about making your mark, however small, on our shared human experience.

As you continue to explore and express yourself, you'll find that your creative endeavors start to influence other areas of your life, including your style. The colors you're drawn to in your art might find their way into your wardrobe, or the themes of your writing might reflect in the accessories you choose. This seamless blend of creativity and personal expression makes you uniquely you. It's a process of discovery, one where each day offers a new canvas to explore.

FASHION AND PERSONAL STYLE

Fashion and personal style are powerful languages of self-expression. This isn't just about the clothes you wear; it's about the story you choose to tell the world about who you are and what you stand for. Your style is an extension of your identity, a visual dialogue that speaks volumes before you even say a word. It's okay if you're not into fashion; skip to the next section. But if this is something that interests you, read on.

Trends that come and go with the seasons. Yet, amidst this dynamic landscape, the most important voice to listen to is your own. It's easy to feel pressured to follow what's popular or mirror the style of influencers and celebrities. But true style is about authenticity, not imitation. It's about making choices that align with your aesthetic, values, and comfort.

Start by exploring what you genuinely love, not just what you think you should wear. Do you feel most empowered in sneakers and a tee, or does your confidence soar in a flowy dress and ballet flats? Your wardrobe should be a curated collection of pieces that make you feel like the best version of yourself. The goal is not to dress for others but to dress for you.

Experimentation can help you discover your unique style. Feel free to mix and match different textures, patterns, and colors. Fashion is an art form, and you are the artist. Some of your experiments may not turn out as expected, and that's perfectly okay. Each misstep is a learning experience, guiding you closer to what makes you feel comfortable and confident.

Accessorizing is another avenue to express your individuality. Accessories like jewelry, scarves, hats, and bags can add a personal touch to any outfit, transforming it from ordinary to distinctly yours. Even how you wear your hair or the makeup you feel drawn to can be integral to your style.

As you evolve, so will your style. What you love today might not resonate with you a few years later, and that's the beauty of personal growth. Your fashion choices can reflect the changes in your life, interests, and perspectives. Embrace this evolution as a natural part of your journey.

Ultimately, fashion and personal style are more than just clothes; they're about self-expression, confidence, and authenticity. They're about making the outside reflect the inside. So, wear what makes you happy, what makes you feel strong, and what makes you unmistakably you. The most stylish thing you can wear is your confidence.

SPEAKING YOUR MIND

Speaking your mind is a crucial skill that will empower you throughout your life, enabling you to stand up for yourself, share your ideas, and connect deeply with others. It's about finding your voice and having the courage to use it.

Speaking your mind doesn't mean you have to shout the loudest or always be in the spotlight. It's about being true to yourself and expressing your thoughts and feelings in the right way. Whether you're a natural introvert who prefers one-on-one conversations or someone who feels at home addressing a crowd, your voice matters.

First, understand that your opinions and feelings are valid. It's okay to have a different viewpoint from your friends or family. What's important is how you communicate these differences. Approach conversations with respect and openness, and you'll find that people are more receptive to hearing what you say.

Listening is just as important as speaking. Paying attention to others shows that you value their opinions, making them more likely to respect yours. It's a two-way street that builds mutual understanding and respect.

Sometimes, speaking your mind can be intimidating, especially when you feel outnumbered or less experienced. Everyone has been there at some point. Start small. Practice expressing your thoughts in less daunting settings, like family dinners or with a close friend. As you build confidence, you'll find it easier to speak up in more challenging situations.

Conflict is a part of life but doesn't have to be negative. When you disagree with someone, see it as an opportunity to explore different perspectives. Keep your cool, use "I" statements to express your feelings, and always strive for a resolution that respects both sides.

Your voice is powerful. It can inspire change, create connections, and lead to personal growth. But it's not just about talking. It's also about reflecting on your experiences and emotions, which is where the power of journaling comes in. By writing down your thoughts and feelings, you gain clarity and discover more about who you are and what you stand for. This self-reflection is a vital part of finding and using your voice effectively.

Speaking your mind is about continuous learning, growing, and embracing every part of yourself. Your voice is unique, and the world is richer for having it. Speak your truth, and let it guide you through life.

THE POWER OF JOURNALING

Once you've started to understand the power of speaking your mind, another equally transformative tool awaits you: journaling. This practice, often underestimated, is a great way to deepen your understanding of yourself and navigate the complex world of emotions and thoughts you'll experience in your teens.

Journaling is more than just keeping a diary. It's a method of self-exploration, a way to document your journey, and a strategy for coping with the rollercoaster of emotions that can sometimes overwhelm you. Think of your journal as a safe space, a reliable friend who is always there to listen without judgment. It's a place to express your deepest fears, highest hopes, and everything in between.

The beauty of journaling lies in its simplicity and accessibility. All you need is a notebook and a pen, or a digital device if you prefer typing over writing by hand. There are no rules to follow or expectations to meet. You can write daily, weekly, or just when you feel like it. What matters is that you're checking in with yourself, acknowledging your feelings and thoughts, and reflecting on your experiences.

One of the most powerful aspects of journaling is its ability to serve as a mirror, reflecting the parts of yourself that you might not always see. Through writing, you can uncover patterns in your thoughts and behaviors, recognize your strengths and areas for growth, and make connections between your feelings and how you react to different situations. This self-awareness can help you grow into the woman you aspire to be.

Journaling also offers a unique form of emotional release. It can be incredibly therapeutic to pour your feelings onto the page, write about what's bothering you, or celebrate your achievements. Sometimes, writing down a problem can make it seem more manageable, and solutions may become more apparent. It's a way to declutter your mind, relieve stress, and enhance your mental well-being.

Your journal can become a collection of memories and insights. Years from now, you'll be able to look back and see how much you've grown, the challenges you've overcome, and the moments of joy that have peppered your journey. It's a record of your resilience, a reflection of your evolving identity, and a reminder of the dreams you're chasing.

In embracing journaling, you're not just documenting your life but actively participating in your own story. You're taking control of your narrative, learning from your experiences, and setting the stage for personal growth. So, grab a notebook and let the pages become a safe place for your thoughts and dreams. Your voice is your most powerful tool, and your journal is the perfect place to let it soar.

CHAPTER SUMMARY

- Discovering your passions is integral to self-expression, exploring what excites and fulfills you, and reflecting your unique identity.
- Curiosity and an open mind are essential in finding your passions. Experimentation with new activities and hobbies can encourage you to uncover the things you enjoy most and discover new passions.
- Acknowledging that passions can evolve and listening to your inner voice is important. Follow genuine interests rather than conforming to external expectations or popular trends.
- Sharing passions with others can be rewarding, as can creating connections and finding a community that shares similar interests or appreciates your enthusiasm.
- Beyond traditional arts, creative outlets offer ways to express your individuality and navigate life's complexities.

- Fashion and personal style are powerful forms of self-expression, showing your authenticity and the evolution of your aesthetic preferences over time.
- Journaling is a powerful and transformative tool for self-reflection, emotional exploration, and documenting personal growth, serving as a private space for self-expression.

CHAPTER 9
UNDERSTANDING MONEY

Money is more than just paper and coins. When used wisely, it's a tool that can help you achieve your dreams and secure your future. Understanding money is the first step toward financial literacy.

Let's start with the basics: money is a medium of exchange. It's what we use to buy the things we need and want. But its value goes beyond the physical; it's also about the choices and opportunities it represents. Every dollar you spend or save is a decision about your priorities and future.

Earning money is often the first step in your financial journey. Whether it's a part-time job, an allowance, or a birthday gift, the moment you start to earn money is when you begin to have control over your financial destiny. It's exciting, isn't it? But with great power comes great responsibility. It's not just about how much you earn but how you manage what you have.

Spending your money wisely is just as important as earning. It's easy to get caught up in the moment and spend all you have on things that bring immediate joy, but remember, every purchase is a trade-off. Ask yourself: Is this something I need, or is it a want? Understanding the difference is crucial. Needs are essentials, like food and shelter, while wants can enhance our lives but aren't necessary for survival.

Now, let's talk about the value of money. Not all dollars are created equal. The value of money changes over time due to inflation, which means that what a dollar buys today might not be the same as what it buys tomorrow. This is why simply saving money under your mattress isn't the best strategy for long-term financial health. Your money needs to grow to keep up with or outpace inflation.

This brings us to the concept of interest. When you save money in a bank, the bank pays you interest, which is a percentage of your savings added to your account over time. This is how your money grows. Similarly, when you borrow money, you pay interest to the lender. Understanding how interest works is key to making informed decisions about saving and borrowing.

Financial literacy is not just about managing money; it's about empowering yourself to make informed decisions that align with your values and goals. Every choice you make with your money reflects what's important to you. Whether saving for college, buying your first car, or supporting a cause you believe in, how you use your money can shape your life and the world around you.

In the next section, we'll dive deeper into the concepts of saving and budgeting. These essential skills will help you build a solid financial foundation. Understanding money is just the beginning. The real magic happens when you use this knowledge to create a future that excites and fulfills you.

SAVING AND BUDGETING

Welcome to the world of saving and budgeting, crucial concepts in your journey to financial literacy. Now that you have a grasp on the basics of money, it's time to dive into how to make it work for you, ensuring a future where financial stress is minimized and your dreams are well within reach.

Saving: Your Financial Safety Net

Think of saving money as building a safety net or a cushion that can catch you when life throws unexpected expenses your way. It's not just about stashing away cash for the sake of it; it's about giving yourself the freedom and security to navigate life's ups and downs with confidence.

Start small. Even a few dollars saved from a weekly allowance or a part-time job can add up over time. Consider opening a savings account if you haven't already, one that earns interest, so your money grows as it sits. Set a goal for something you want to save for: a new phone, college fund, or even a trip with friends. Having a tangible goal can make saving feel more rewarding.

Budgeting: Your Financial Blueprint

Budgeting, on the other hand, is about planning how to spend your money wisely. A budget guides you in allocating your money to cover your needs, wants, and savings goals. Creating a budget helps you see where your money is going, making it easier to make adjustments and avoid overspending.

To start, list your income sources, such as allowances, gifts, or any earnings from part-time jobs. Then, list your expenses, categorizing them into needs (like school supplies or transportation) and wants (such as eating out with friends or buying new clothes). Don't forget to include a category for savings – it's a crucial part of your budget.

Once you have everything laid out, see where you can make adjustments to increase your savings. Maybe you can reduce some of your wants to boost your savings. Or perhaps you'll find creative ways to increase your income, like taking on extra chores or selling items you no longer need.

Thankfully, you don't have to do all this with pen and paper. Numerous apps and online tools can help you track your savings and manage your budget. These tools can provide insights into your spending habits, helping you make informed decisions about your money.

The goal of saving and budgeting isn't to restrict your life but to enhance it. By mastering these skills, you're setting yourself up for a future where financial worries are less of a burden and your dreams are just a well-planned step away.

SMART SPENDING

Smart spending is more than avoiding overspending or being stingy to the point of deprivation. Instead, it's about making informed choices that align with your values and goals, ensuring each dollar you spend is a step toward the future you envision for yourself.

Imagine you're at the mall, your wallet a silent witness to the transactions about to unfold. Before you let the excitement of a sale or the allure of a new item sweep you away, pause and ask yourself: "Do I really need this?" This simple question can be a powerful tool in your smart spending toolkit. It encourages you to differentiate between wants and needs. This distinction can lead to more mindful and satisfying spending habits.

But smart spending doesn't stop at questioning your purchases. It also involves doing your homework. In today's digital age, comparing prices, reading reviews, and seeking the best deals has never been easier. A little research can go a long way in ensuring you get the most bang for your buck. Whether waiting for a sale, using a coupon, or choosing a less expensive alternative, these strategies can help you maintain your budget without sacrificing quality or enjoyment.

Another aspect of smart spending is understanding the true cost of a purchase. This includes considering the item's lifespan and any additional expenses it may incur, such as maintenance or accessories. For example, buying a cheaper gadget that breaks down after a few months may cost more in the long run than investing in a slightly more expensive but more durable option.

Smart spending is not just about saving money; it's also about investing in experiences and items that truly add value to your life. Perhaps allocating part of your budget to a hobby that brings you joy or saving for a trip that will create lasting memories is worth more than a closet full of hardly worn clothes.

Every spending decision you make today shapes your financial future tomorrow. By spending wisely, you're safeguarding your financial well-being and laying the groundwork for a future where financial stress is minimized and financial freedom is within reach.

The principles of smart spending will serve as a foundation upon which you can build more complex financial strategies. It's about creating a balance that allows you to enjoy the present while preparing for the future—a future that, with careful planning and wise financial decisions, is bright and full of promise.

PLANNING FOR THE FUTURE

The next step is to look ahead and plan for the future. This isn't about predicting what will happen but preparing yourself to navigate whatever comes your way confidently.

Planning for the future involves setting financial goals. These can be short-term goals, like saving up for a concert ticket or a new outfit, or long-term goals, such as funding your college education. Start with what matters to you most and then break down these goals into achievable steps.

One effective way to plan is by creating a budget that includes savings. Think of your savings as a bill you pay your future self. It may seem odd to think about paying yourself, but this mindset shift can make all the difference. Each time you save, you invest in your future dreams and well-being.

Another aspect of planning for the future is understanding the power of compound interest. It's the concept of earning interest on your interest and how a small amount of money can grow over time. For example, if you start saving a small amount regularly at a young age, you could end up with a significant sum by the time you're ready to retire, thanks to compound interest.

It's also wise to educate yourself about different financial products and services to help you achieve your goals. This includes savings accounts, certificates of deposit, and investment options like stocks, bonds, and mutual funds. Each of these comes with its rules, risks, and potential rewards. The more you know, the better decisions you'll be able to make.

Planning for the future also means being prepared for the unexpected. This includes having an emergency fund to cover unexpected expenses, especially if you live out of home. While it might seem like a lot, starting small and building up gradually can make it more manageable.

As you move forward, remember that planning for the future is not a one-time task but an ongoing process. Your goals and circumstances will change, and so should your plans. By staying informed, making thoughtful decisions, and adjusting as needed, you can confidently navigate your financial future. Every step you take now is a step towards a more secure and fulfilling future.

EARNING YOUR OWN MONEY

Earning your own money is a pivotal step in growing up. It's not just about having cash to spend on the things you love or saving for something big. It's about understanding the value of hard work, gaining a sense of responsibility, and learning how to manage your finances. So, let's dive into some practical ways to earn money and the lessons you'll learn.

Consider part-time jobs or internships that align with your interests or future career aspirations. Whether it's working in a local café, bookstore, or even an internship at a company, these opportunities not only provide you with a paycheck but also invaluable work experience. You'll learn about the importance of punctuality, teamwork, and customer service—essential skills in any career path.

Another avenue to explore is freelancing or starting your own small business. Are you good at graphic design, writing, or coding? Platforms like Fiverr and Upwork allow you to offer your skills to a global audience. Perhaps you're crafty and can sell handmade goods on Etsy. These paths can teach you about entrepreneurship, marketing, and the satisfaction of earning from your creativity.

If you love spending time with children or pets, babysitting or pet sitting are great options. These jobs require high trust and responsibility, teaching you about caring for others and managing your time effectively. Plus, they can be quite rewarding, both financially and personally.

Don't forget about leveraging technology to earn. From taking online surveys to tutoring students online, there are numerous ways to make money from the comfort of your home. This provides flexibility and introduces you to the digital economy, a critical aspect of our modern world.

As you start to earn your own money, remember to set financial goals and budget wisely. It's tempting to spend your hard-earned cash impulsively, but learning to save and invest part of your earnings will set you up for long-term success. Consider opening a savings account or learning about basic investing. These steps secure your financial future and empower you to make informed decisions with your money.

Earning your own money is an exciting and empowering process. It's about more than just the paycheck; it's about the skills you develop, the confidence you gain, and the lessons you learn about the value of money. So, take that step forward, explore the opportunities around you, and embrace the journey toward financial literacy and independence.

CHAPTER SUMMARY

- Financial literacy begins with understanding money as a tool for achieving your dreams and securing your future, acknowledging the importance of wise spending and saving.
- Money is a medium of exchange, representing choices and opportunities, with each dollar spent or saved reflecting personal priorities and plans.
- Earning money through jobs, allowances, or gifts marks the start of your financial independence and highlights the responsibility of managing your finances well.
- Wise spending involves distinguishing between needs and wants, understanding the impact of each purchase on financial goals, and considering the long-term value of money due to inflation.
- Saving money in accounts that earn interest and understanding the role of interest in growing savings and borrowing costs are integral concepts of financial literacy.

- Financial literacy empowers you to make informed decisions that align with your values and goals.
- Budgeting and saving are foundational skills for money management. Budgeting acts as a plan for allocating resources and saving as a safety net for your future needs and goals.
- Earning your own money through part-time jobs, freelancing, or small businesses teaches the value of hard work, responsibility, and the importance of managing your money wisely.

CHAPTER 10
THE WORLD AROUND YOU

In a world that's more connected than ever, understanding global issues is not just about being aware; it's about recognizing the role you play in a global community. It's easy to feel small or disconnected from problems that seem to happen far away or to others. However, the truth is that everything from the environment to economics, from social justice to scientific advancements, affects us all in some way. This interconnectedness means that you can make choices that contribute positively to the world by being informed.

First, let's talk about the environment. Climate change is a global issue that impacts everything from weather patterns to food production and sea levels. Understanding the science behind climate change and the actions that contribute to it is the first step in being part of the solution. Simple actions like reducing waste, conserving water, and supporting sustainable products and practices can make a difference.

Social justice is another critical area. Around the world, people are fighting for their rights, whether for gender equality, racial equality, or the rights of LGBTQ+ individuals. By educating yourself on these issues, you can become an ally supporting equality and fairness locally and globally. This might involve participating in or organizing awareness campaigns, supporting relevant nonprofits, or standing up against injustice in your community.

Economic issues also play a significant role in our interconnected world. Understanding the basics of how economies operate, the significance of trade, and the impact of poverty can help you grasp the complexities of global economics. This knowledge can guide your choices as a consumer and inform your views on policies that affect global economic stability and growth.

Lastly, staying informed about scientific advancements and health issues is crucial. From developing new technologies to spreading diseases, science impacts our lives in countless ways. By understanding these developments, you can make informed decisions about your health, advocate for science-based policies, and appreciate the role of innovation in solving global problems.

Being an informed citizen means continuously learning, questioning the information you come across, and thinking critically about how you can contribute to positive change. It's about empathy, understanding, and action. Your daily choices, no matter how small they seem, can have a global impact. By staying informed and engaged, you're not just preparing yourself to navigate the world but shaping it for the better.

BEING AN INFORMED CITIZEN

Being an informed citizen is about understanding the happenings around you, locally and globally, and recognizing how they can impact your life and the lives of others. This journey of awareness is not just about staying updated through news headlines; it's about developing a deeper understanding of the issues and learning how to engage with them thoughtfully.

Firstly, let's talk about the importance of diverse sources. In an age where information is at our fingertips, it's easy to fall into the trap of echo chambers, where the news we consume only reinforces our existing beliefs. Challenge yourself to explore a variety of news outlets, including those with differing viewpoints. This will broaden your perspective and help you develop critical thinking skills. It will enable you to differentiate between fact and opinion and recognize bias when you see it.

Understanding the issues is one thing, but engaging with them is another. Engaging doesn't necessarily mean you have to lead a protest or write op-eds (though those are fantastic ways to make your voice heard if you wish). It can be as simple as discussing current events with friends and family, thereby fostering a culture of awareness and dialogue in your immediate circles. Every big change starts with small conversations.

In the digital age, social media platforms have become

powerful tools for advocacy and change. They offer a space to share information, join communities with similar interests, and even mobilize for causes you care about. However, it's essential to navigate these spaces responsibly. Always verify the information before sharing it, respect others' opinions, and remember that a human is behind every screen.

The world is constantly changing, and with it, the issues that shape our society. Stay curious, ask questions, and never underestimate the power of knowledge. Your voice matters, and by staying informed, you're preparing yourself to participate in the world around you and laying the groundwork for a more informed, empathetic, and engaged society.

Knowledge is not just for keeping; it's for sharing and acting upon. The next step involves taking the awareness you've cultivated to make a difference in the world. Whether through volunteering, advocacy, or simply lending a helping hand, your actions, informed by your understanding of the world, can create ripples of change.

VOLUNTEERING AND GIVING BACK

In our bustling world, it's easy to get caught up in our own lives, routines, and the digital whirlwind that constantly surrounds us. However, a beautiful, enriching aspect of life beckons us to step outside of our comfort zones and personal bubbles: volunteering and giving back to our communities. This service is not just about helping others; it's a pathway to personal growth, understanding, and connection that enriches our lives in ways we might not expect.

Volunteering allows you to see the world through a different lens, often filled with gratitude, compassion, and a deeper understanding of the diversity of human experience. It's about making a difference in someone else's life, no matter how small. Whether tutoring children at a local school, spending time with older people in nursing homes, or participating in community clean-up projects, each act of service contributes to a larger picture of kindness and community.

But how do you start? Begin by identifying causes that matter to you. Are you passionate about animal welfare, environmental conservation, or perhaps advocating for people experiencing homelessness? Once you have pinpointed your interests, research local organizations or groups that align with those causes. Volunteering doesn't have to be a solo experience. You could involve your friends or family members. Not only does this amplify the impact of your efforts, but it also creates shared experiences that can strengthen your relationships.

One of the most beautiful aspects of volunteering is the mutual exchange. While you're giving your time, energy, and skills, you're also receiving. You gain new perspectives, develop empathy, and often learn new skills. These experiences can shape your worldview, influence future career choices, and even guide your values and beliefs.

Giving back to your community can foster a sense of belonging and connection. In a world where we're often divided by screens and distances, volunteering offers a unique opportunity to connect with others face-to-face and to work alongside people from different backgrounds and walks of life towards a common goal. This sense of community is invaluable, reminding us that, despite our differences, we share common hopes, dreams, and challenges.

Every small action counts. You don't need to move mountains to make a difference. Often, the smallest gestures of kindness and generosity leave the most significant impact. So, take that step, reach out, and discover the joy and fulfillment of serving others. In doing so, you're not just changing the world around you but also transforming yourself.

ENVIRONMENTAL AWARENESS

Understanding and engaging with the environment around you is not just a responsibility—it's a journey of discovery and empowerment. As you step out of the realm of volunteering and giving back, you carry with you the desire to make a difference, which goes hand in hand with environmental awareness.

The environment is the air you breathe, the water you drink, and the ground on which all life dances. Your relationship with the environment is personal and profound; recognizing this connection is the first step toward living in harmony with the earth.

Start with the small, everyday choices that paint the larger picture of your impact on the planet. Consider the products you use, from the clothes you wear to the food you eat. Are they sourced in a way that respects the environment and the people who produce them? The power of your wallet is real—supporting businesses and initiatives that prioritize sustainability sends a powerful message and contributes to positive change.

But environmental awareness is not just about what you buy; it's also about what you do. Reducing waste, conserving water, and minimizing your carbon footprint are within your reach. Simple habits like carrying a reusable water bottle, using public transportation, or even biking to your destinations can significantly impact you over time. These choices benefit the planet and often lead to a healthier, more mindful lifestyle.

Beyond personal actions, your voice is a powerful tool for environmental advocacy. Whether through art, social media, or conversations with friends and family, expressing your concerns and hopes for the environment can inspire others to take notice and act. Change often starts with a single voice that can grow into a chorus calling for action.

The challenges facing our planet are complex, but they are not unconquerable, especially when faced with your generation's creativity and passion. Embrace this journey with an open heart and mind, ready to learn, adapt, and make a difference.

As you prepare to step into the next chapter of your life, remember that the world is vast and filled with cultures and perspectives that can enrich your understanding of environmental issues. Traveling and cultural exploration offer unique opportunities to see firsthand the global impact of environmental choices and how communities worldwide work toward sustainability. Your journey of environmental awareness is not just about making a difference in your corner of the world; it's about joining a global community of change-makers united in their respect and care for the planet.

TRAVELING AND CULTURAL EXPLORATION

Traveling can be one of the most enlightening experiences of your teenage years as you embrace different cultures and diverse landscapes. Traveling and cultural exploration open doors to understanding the world around you and yourself in ways you might never have imagined.

Embarking on travels, whether to a bustling city a few hours away or a tranquil village on the other side of the globe, invites new experiences. You may taste foods that dance on your tongue with unfamiliar flavors, hear melodies and languages that are as intriguing as they are foreign, and see sights that broaden your perspective and challenge your perceptions.

However, as thrilling as exploration can be, it's also essential to approach it with a sense of responsibility and awareness. Remember, you're not just a visitor but a guest. Respecting local customs, traditions, and etiquette is important. Before you go, take the time to learn about the dos and don'ts, the cultural nuances, and even a few phrases in the local language. It's a sign of respect that can open hearts and doors, making your experience all the more enriching.

Safety is another crucial aspect of traveling, especially for young women. Always research your destination thoroughly, understanding the safest areas to stay and explore and the local laws and regulations. Share your travel plans with someone you trust, keep your belongings secure, and always listen to your intuition. If something doesn't feel right, trust that feeling.

Traveling is also an opportunity to practice sustainability and environmental consciousness in new settings. Choosing eco-friendly accommodations, supporting local businesses, and minimizing your carbon footprint are ways to give back to the places that give so much to us in terms of experiences and memories.

Lastly, keep an open mind when you travel. The beauty of travel lies in its ability to surprise and challenge us. Not every experience will be comfortable, but growth often lies in discomfort. Embrace the unexpected, learn from every encounter, and let these experiences shape you into a more empathetic and knowledgeable woman.

As you explore the world, each place you travel to is a new chapter in your story. Travel with curiosity, respect, and an open heart, and watch as the world unfolds its wonders.

CHAPTER SUMMARY

- Understanding global issues is crucial in a connected world, and you have the power to understand and get involved in global challenges.
- Environmental awareness involves understanding climate change and taking actions like reducing waste and supporting sustainable practices.
- Social justice issues, including gender, racial, and LGBTQ+ rights, require education and active support to promote equality and fairness.
- Economic knowledge helps you grasp the complexities of global economics, guides your own consumer choices, and helps you form views on policies affecting economic stability.
- Staying informed about scientific advancements and health issues enables you to make informed health decisions and support science-based policies.
- Being an informed citizen involves seeking diverse news sources, engaging in discussions, and using social media responsibly for advocacy.
- Volunteering and giving back enriches personal growth and community connection.
- Travel and cultural exploration enhances your understanding of yourself and the world. It's essential to respect the places you travel to, travel safely, and practice environmental consciousness.

CHAPTER 11
CAREER EXPLORATION AND PLANNING FOR THE FUTURE

Exploring what you'd like to do after school can be thrilling and overwhelming at the same time. But don't worry! This chapter will help steer you through this process with confidence and clarity.

First, let's talk about career exploration. Understanding yourself is the first step to deciding what career path you'd like to take. What lights a fire in your heart? Is it the thought of crafting beautiful stories, designing skyscrapers, or perhaps unraveling the mysteries of the universe? Your passions are powerful indicators of where your career path might lead. It's perfectly okay if you're still figuring it out. Exploration is part of the adventure.

Think about your skills and strengths. You may have a knack for solving complex problems, or your superpower lies in connecting with people. Recognizing these abilities can help you identify careers that align with what you naturally excel at. Don't shy away from seeking feedback from teachers, family, and friends. Sometimes, they can spot talents you didn't even know you had.

Research plays a crucial role in career exploration. The internet is a library of information. Dive into job descriptions, watch day-in-the-life videos of professionals in various fields, and read up on future job trends. This can help you understand what a day on the job looks like and what skills you'll need.

Networking isn't just for adults. Start building your network now by connecting with mentors, attending workshops, and joining clubs that align with your interests. These connections can offer invaluable advice, expose you to new opportunities, and even help you land your first job or internship.

Career exploration is a dynamic process, not a race. Changing your mind, exploring different paths, and even taking a few detours is okay. What's important is that you remain curious, open to new experiences, and true to yourself.

Remember that the decisions you make today are not set in stone. They are stepping stones towards a future that's uniquely yours. Embrace the process with an open heart and an adventurous spirit. The world is full of possibilities, and your path is yours to shape.

THE COLLEGE DECISION

Embarking on the college decision journey is a significant milestone, marking the transition from the familiar world of high school to the expansive horizons of higher education and beyond. This is not just about choosing a place to study; it's about aligning your dreams, passions, and goals with the environment that will nurture and challenge you to grow.

There is no one-size-fits-all approach to selecting a college. What works well for a friend or sibling may not be the best fit for you, and that's perfectly okay. Your college decision should reflect who you are and aspire to become. It's a deeply personal choice that deserves careful thought and consideration.

Start by reflecting on your career exploration journey. What fields or subjects sparked a fire in you? Consider colleges that offer strong programs in those areas. Do your research – delve into course catalogs, faculty qualifications, and the opportunities for hands-on experience through internships or research projects. The program's quality is more important than the college's prestige.

Financial considerations are also important. College is a significant investment in your future, but it shouldn't be a burden that weighs you down with debt for decades. Explore scholarships, grants, and work-study programs. Be open to considering community colleges or state universities, which can offer an excellent education at a more affordable cost. Sometimes, starting at a community college and then transferring to a four-year institution can be a smart financial strategy without compromising the quality of your education.

Campus culture and environment play a significant role in your college experience. Do you thrive in a bustling, urban campus, or do you prefer the close-knit community of a smaller college? Consider the location, size, and social atmosphere of the campus. Visit if you can, attend information sessions, and connect with current students to get a feel for the day-to-day campus life.

Listen to your heart and engage your head as you go through this process. It's easy to be influenced by others' opinions or the allure of a prestigious name. But, at the end of the day, you're the one who will be walking this path. Trust yourself, and don't be afraid to take the road less traveled if it feels right for you. You may not even decide to go to a traditional college. Many alternative higher education options are available, such as apprenticeships and training and vocational colleges.

Your college decision is not the be-all and end-all. It's a significant step, but it's just one of many you'll take on your journey to independence and adulthood. Embrace the process with an open mind and a resilient spirit. The choices you make now are important, but they're not irreversible. Life is full of opportunities to pivot, grow, and change direction.

As you progress from making your college decision, the next section will explore life skills that will support your independence and success in college. From managing your finances to caring for your physical and mental health, the journey ahead is more than academic achievement; it's about becoming a well-rounded, empowered woman ready to take on the world.

LIFE SKILLS FOR INDEPENDENCE

As you stand on the brink of adulthood, the world stretches before you like a vast, uncharted map. It's thrilling, yes, but also a bit daunting. How do you navigate this new terrain? How do you ensure that you're not just surviving but thriving? The key lies in arming yourself with essential life skills that encourage you to be independent. These skills are your compass that can help guide you through the wilderness of the real world.

Financial Literacy

First and foremost, financial literacy is non-negotiable, and we explored this earlier in the book. Understanding how to manage your money can feel like learning a new language—the language of adulthood. Start with the basics: budgeting, saving, and understanding credit. Create a budget that accounts for your income (no matter how small) and expenses. Learn the art of saving—a little can go a long way. And when it comes to credit, know it's a double-edged sword. Used wisely, it can be a tool for building a future; used recklessly, it can lead to a mountain of debt.

Self-Care

Next, let's talk about self-care. It's a term thrown around often, but at its core, self-care is about caring for your physical and mental health. This means eating nutritious foods, getting enough sleep, exercising regularly, and finding healthy ways to cope with stress. Your health is your wealth. Without it, all the success in the world means little.

Cooking

Cooking is another invaluable skill. Something is empowering about being able to nourish yourself with meals you've prepared.

Start simple. Learn to cook a handful of healthy, budget-friendly dishes. Cooking is not just about feeding your body; it's about feeding your soul, too.

Digital Literacy

In today's digital age, understanding technology is crucial. From creating a professional-looking resume to managing your digital footprint, tech-savviness can open doors. It's not just about being able to navigate social media or use a smartphone; it's about understanding how to leverage technology to your advantage in both your personal and professional life.

Effective Communication

Effective communication is a skill that's appeared in numerous chapters of this book. Whether negotiating a salary, resolving conflicts, or simply expressing your needs, communicating clearly and confidently is a superpower. It's about listening as much as it is about speaking. The most successful people are not just great talkers but also great listeners.

Don't worry if you don't have these skills mastered right away. You'll get better at them over time, and there are lots of resources to help you learn and practice them. As you venture into the world, remember that independence is not about doing everything independently; it's about having the confidence and the know-how to navigate life's challenges. It's about knowing when to ask for help and when to stand on two feet. So, take these skills, refine them, and make them your own. Your future self will thank you.

As you master these skills, you'll find that they lay the groundwork for the next step in your journey: building a personal brand. This isn't just about how you present yourself online; it's about knowing who you are, what you stand for, and how you communicate that to the world.

BUILDING A PERSONAL BRAND

As you grow up and carve a unique space for yourself in this vast world, understanding the power of a personal brand is like discovering a compass that guides you toward your dreams. It's not just about logos or social media profiles; it's about the essence of who you are, what you stand for, and how you communicate your values to the world. Building a personal brand is crafting your story in a way that resonates with others, making meaningful and beneficial connections.

Being genuine is your greatest asset in a world full of filters and facades. Your personal brand should reflect your true self, not someone you think others will like. It's about embracing your quirks, passions, and unique life perspective. When you are authentic, you attract people who appreciate the real you, whether in friendships, in the classroom, or, one day, in the workplace.

Next, consider your passions and values. What gets you the most excited in life? Is it environmental activism, digital art, writing, or something entirely different? Your personal brand should weave these passions and values into a coherent narrative. This doesn't mean you need to have all the answers now. It's okay for your interests to evolve. What's important is that you're exploring and expressing what matters to you.

How you express yourself, both online and offline, plays a significant role in building your personal brand. It's not just about what you say but how you say it. Being mindful of your words and actions, showing kindness, and respecting others' opinions will help you build a positive reputation. Every post and interaction is a brushstroke in the bigger picture of your personal brand.

Networking is another crucial aspect. Building a network of supportive friends, mentors, and professionals can open doors to opportunities you never knew existed. Attend workshops, join clubs related to your interests, be bold, and reach out to people you admire. These connections can guide, inspire, and support you as you navigate your path.

Building a personal brand requires patience, persistence, and a lot of self-reflection. There will be moments of doubt, uncertainty, and incredible growth and discovery. Embrace every step of this adventure, knowing that you're building a brand and laying the foundation for the future you dream of.

Keep your eyes on the horizon, dream big, and set goals that challenge you to overcome your fears and doubts. Your personal brand is the first step in a journey of a thousand miles that promises adventure, growth, and endless possibilities.

DREAMING BIG

Dreaming big is not just about wishful thinking; it's a powerful tool for setting the stage for your future. It's about envisioning a life that excites you, motivates you, and pushes you to explore what's possible.

Dreaming big starts with understanding that your aspirations are valid, no matter how majestic they may seem. Whether you dream of becoming an astronaut, a world-renowned artist, or a leader in social change, your dreams are the blueprint for your future. They are the first step in creating a life that aligns with your passions, values, and strengths.

However, dreaming big is not just about the end goal but also the process. It involves recognizing the steps you need to take to get there and being open to opportunities and experiences that come your way. It's about resilience in the face of challenges and setbacks, knowing that each obstacle is a stepping stone closer to your dream.

Start by giving yourself permission to explore all your interests and passions without judgment. Write them down, no matter how quirky or unconventional they may seem. Then, think about what steps you can take now, no matter how small, to move closer to those dreams. This could be as simple as joining a club related to your interests, seeking out a mentor, or dedicating time each week to learn something new that brings you closer to your goal.

The power of dreaming big lies not just in achieving your dreams but also in the person you become along the way. It's about growing, learning, and pushing beyond your comfort zone. Let your personal brand guide you in making decisions that align with who you are and who you aspire to be.

So, dream big. Let your dreams be the star that guides you through the adventure of planning for your future. Embrace the possibilities, for in dreaming big, you open the door to a world of opportunities waiting to be explored.

CHAPTER SUMMARY

- Career exploration involves understanding your passions and skills to help guide you down your chosen career path.
- Research and networking can help you identify potential career paths and gain insights into various professions. Adopt an open-minded approach to career exploration, allowing for changes in direction and the pursuit of diverse interests.
- The college decision process is deeply personal; consider your passions, financial implications, and campus culture when choosing where to go after high school. Select a college based on program quality over prestige.
- Explore financial aid options to help minimize college debt. Don't be afraid to look into alternative higher education options if a traditional college isn't right for you.
- Life skills such as financial literacy, self-care, cooking, digital literacy, and effective communication are essential for independence and success.
- Your personal brand should reflect your true self, passions, and values.
- Dreaming big is a powerful tool for setting future goals. Be open to opportunities and resilient in the face of challenges.

YOUR STORY CONTINUES

As you're about to start a new chapter in your life, it's a good time to think about everything you've been through to get here. It's not just about remembering the past but also about seeing how much you've grown, the obstacles you've overcome, and the inner strength you've developed. Each step, stumble, and triumph is a building block that has helped form who you are today.

Think about all your experiences, even the small or tough ones, because they have shaped your unique story. It's important to see the value in the hard times because that's when you discover how strong, brave, and determined you are.

Remember when you were challenged or pushed out of your comfort zone? Those moments taught you a lot about yourself and the world. They showed you how resilient you are and that you can face challenges head-on. Instead of seeing problems as dead ends, you've learned to view them as steps toward becoming the best version of yourself.

Remember the people who've been part of your journey, too. The mentors, friends, and even those who doubted you helped shape your path. They've taught you valuable lessons about trust, friendship, and believing in yourself.

This moment of reflection isn't the end but a chance to appreciate how far you've come and prepare for what's next. It's a time to gather the lessons learned, strength gained, and wisdom acquired as you prepare to move forward. With every experience, you're more prepared for the future, seeing it not as a bunch of hurdles but as a world full of opportunities.

So, be proud of how far you've come. The challenges you've faced have set you up for the exciting adventures that are yet to come. Your story is just starting, and with your dreams and the strength you've gained, you're ready to take on whatever comes your way.

EMBRACING YOUR TEENAGE YEARS

The adventure ahead is all about finding new things and understanding yourself better. Your journey is unique and filled with learning, fun, tears, and victories. Now, as you get ready for what comes next, it's time to use the wisdom you've gained and be open to new things.

Preparing for the next part of your life means accepting that change is necessary for growth. It's about seeing the unknown not as something scary but as exciting and full of possibilities. You might face new challenges, but like before, you can overcome them and become even stronger.

Consider this new chapter a fresh start in your life's story. It's your chance to try different things, set exciting goals, and build on your achievements. Your past has given you a set of tools for the future; now, it's up to you to choose how to use them.

Embracing your teenage years doesn't mean you need all the answers immediately. It's about being willing to learn, grow, and change. It's about making choices that show who you are and want to be. Every day gives you a chance to shape your story, make decisions that match your values, and live in a way that makes you happy and fulfilled.

On this journey, it's important to have people who support and lift you up. Look for mentors, friends, and groups that help you grow and respect who you are. These relationships will help guide, offer new views, and encourage you as you face life's ups and downs.

Be kind to yourself as you progress, celebrate every win, and learn from tough times. Your journey isn't a race; it's a beautiful, ongoing story where every experience, choice, and lesson adds to your life's rich story.

So, take a deep breath, believe in yourself, and step forward with confidence. The next chapter is waiting, full of possibilities, and it's yours to create with purpose, strength, and grace.

STAYING TRUE TO YOURSELF

Always remember who you are. Even when life gets crazy with changes and challenges, staying true to yourself is super important. It's the light that will illuminate your path forward in life.

Being true to yourself sounds easy, but it's pretty complicated, as you've probably already learned. It's about knowing what you stand for, understanding your strengths, and being okay with your weaknesses. It's making choices that feel right to you, even if it means not following everyone else or what's expected by society or those around you.

Your uniqueness is your special power. The world doesn't need a copy of someone else; it needs the real you, with all your unique traits and dreams. Embrace your quirks, passions, and dreams. Those are the things that make your life your unique masterpiece.

But being true to yourself doesn't mean you never change. You're continually growing and changing. Your interests and beliefs might change over time, and that's fine. Being true to yourself means allowing yourself to try new things, ask questions, and change. It's about listening to your own voice, even as it changes.

In this journey of self-discovery, you'll face challenges that test your strength. You might find yourself in situations where it's tempting to give up on what you believe in or hide who you are. Being strong in your values is like building muscle—the more you stick to them, the stronger you'll get. Stay true to what you believe, even when it's difficult. Your respect for yourself is way more valuable than any quick approval from others.

As you progress through your teens, take all the lessons, love, and strength you've gained from being your true self. The path ahead is yours, and while it might not always be smooth, it's beautiful because it's a life lived honestly. Your story continues, and you're the only one who can write it.

CONTINUING TO GROW AND LEARN

As you go through life, your story might change chapters, but the heart of it stays bright and full of possibilities. Growing and learning isn't a straight path but more like a spiral. You might face similar challenges and joys more than once, but each time you do, you see them with fresh eyes and understand yourself and the world a bit better.

Being open to constantly growing means realizing there's always something new to discover, not just about your hobbies or skills, but about who you are at your core. It's about giving yourself the chance to change, to think differently, and to follow what truly excites you. This journey is yours alone, with its ups and downs, but remember, you're not doing it alone.

Learning isn't just something that happens in school. It's in the quiet moments when you think things over, in tough times, and when you find something that speaks to you. It's in the talks you have, the books you read, and the dreams you chase. Every day is a chance to learn something new about the world, others, and yourself.

As you keep growing, remember the lessons about being strong, kind, and true to yourself that you've picked up along the way. These lessons will help you handle life's challenges with elegance and bravery. They're the seeds for what you'll leave behind—a legacy defined not just by what you've done but by how you've touched others, the love you've spread, and the brightness you've added to the world.

Let your curiosity lead the way on this never-ending adventure of growth and discovery, and your passions drive you. Stay open to new things, and don't be scared to try something out of your comfort zone. The world is vast and full of amazing things to see and understand. And as you keep on growing, remember, your story is still unfolding, one wonderful, courageous, and shining page at a time.

LEAVING A LEGACY

As you go through life, ready to grow and learn, think about the mark you want to leave on the world. It's not about big actions or achievements but about who you are and the small ways you make a difference every day.

Your legacy is in the kindness you show others, the enthusiasm you put into your work, and how you keep going when things get tough. It's in the stories you tell, the laughter you share, and the comfort you give. These actions weave together to create your unique legacy.

Think about what values matter most to you, like kindness, bravery, honesty, or creativity. Consider how these values influence what you do and decide. Your legacy shines through these values, lighting the way for others.

Your legacy changes as you do. Every new experience, challenge, and victory lets you add more to your legacy, making it richer and more colorful. It's a chance to discover more about how you affect others and learn about your own character.

Your legacy also includes how you help others grow and succeed. It's seen in the encouragement you give to a friend, the support you offer when someone needs it, and how you celebrate others' wins as if they were your own. By doing this, you add to your legacy and help others build theirs.

Every moment is a chance to add something beautiful to your life. With every kind act, effort, and challenge faced with dignity, you're not just creating your own story but also contributing to a bigger one filled with hope, strength, and endless possibilities. Your legacy is your unique gift to the world. And you are exactly where you need to be right now. So, embrace your teenage years with excitement and confidence. Believe in yourself—you've got this!

HOW TO EMBRACE YOUR SPARK

A SELF-LOVE GUIDE FOR TEEN GIRLS TO BUILD CONFIDENCE, BOOST SELF-ESTEEM AND PRACTICE SELF-CARE

EMBRACING YOUR SPARK

Welcome to the beginning of a journey that is entirely your own. This is a journey of discovery, growth, and, most importantly, love—the kind of love that starts with you. It's a path you're not meant to walk alone, but rather, one shared with the wisdom of those who've walked it before and the friendship of those who walk it alongside you.

In the following chapters, we will explore the concept of self-love. Self-love might seem broad and sometimes cliched, but it is as important to your well-being as the air you breathe. Self-love is the basis upon which you build your dreams, the armor that protects you when you doubt yourself, and the light that guides you back home to yourself when the world seems dark.

Loving yourself helps you see what's special about you, empowering you to shine and embrace your individual spark.

Self-love isn't about perfection. It's not a destination you arrive at, declaring victory. Instead, it's about embracing every part of yourself—your strengths, vulnerabilities, successes, and setbacks.

It's about recognizing your worth and value, free from the opinions and thoughts of others.

This journey is about learning to be your best friend, top supporter, and most trusted adviser. It's about setting boundaries that make you happy, pursuing passions you care about, and making choices that reflect your love for yourself.

As we explore the different elements of self-love, know that this journey is uniquely yours. Your path may twist and turn, rise and fall, in ways different from anyone else's. And that's okay. In fact, it's more than okay—it's beautiful. Because it's by navigating these personal experiences that you'll discover your strength and the boundless capacity of your heart to love.

So, take a deep breath and step forward with courage and curiosity. You are about to embark on one of the most important adventures of your life—the journey of loving and celebrating the incredible person that you are.

WHAT IS SELF-LOVE?

Self-love, in simple terms, is a deep acceptance and appreciation of oneself. It's about recognizing your worth, embracing your uniqueness, and nurturing your well-being. It's a journey of understanding that you are enough, just as you are, without needing to prove anything to anyone else. Self-love is not just about feeling good about yourself—it's about treating yourself with kindness, respect, and compassion, especially when you might feel you don't deserve it.

Self-love is a powerful act of defiance in a world that often tries to tell you how to act, look, and dream. It's choosing to honor your feelings, listen to your inner voice, and set boundaries that protect yourself. It's about making choices that reflect what you want rather than what others expect of you.

Self-love is also about recognizing that you are a work in progress and that growth and mistakes are part of the journey. It's understanding that you don't have to be perfect to be worthy of love—especially your own. This means forgiving yourself when you stumble and knowing that every day is a new opportunity to treat yourself better.

Self-love involves taking care of your physical, emotional, and mental health. It's about making time for activities that nourish your soul. It's also about surrounding yourself with people who uplift you and letting go of relationships that drain your energy.

At its core, self-love helps you build an authentic and fulfilling life. It's the light that guides you back to yourself when the world tries to pull you away. While the path to self-love may look different for everyone, the destination is the same: a place of inner peace, strength, and joy.

As you embark on this journey, remember that self-love is not a destination but a practice. It's something you cultivate every day in your choices and how you treat yourself. And though the journey may not always be easy, every step you take towards loving yourself more is a step towards living a more authentic, happy life.

WHY SELF-LOVE MATTERS

In the tapestry of life, each thread represents a unique aspect of who we are, weaving together to form the intricate masterpiece that is you. You control your life, deciding which threads to weave in and which to leave out. It's a time of exploration, of discovering who you are and who you want to become.

Self-love is not just a trendy term; it's the basis upon which you build your sense of self-worth and confidence. But why does it matter so much, especially for you, at this moment in your life?

During your teenage years, you face many pressures, from academic expectations to social conflicts. The world around you seems to be constantly shifting, and with it, the idea of who you're supposed to be. It's easy to get lost in the noise, compare yourself to others, and feel like you're not good enough. This is where self-love steps in as a powerful tool.

Embracing self-love means allowing yourself to be imperfect, make mistakes, and learn from them. It means putting yourself first and prioritizing your mental and physical well-being. When you love yourself, you acknowledge your strengths and weaknesses and accept them as integral parts of your identity. This is the starting point for growth and self-improvement.

Self-love also influences how you interact with the world. It teaches you to value your own opinions and stand up for yourself. It empowers you to follow your own path, rather than one set by societal expectations or peer pressure. When you love yourself, you express confidence and authenticity, attracting positive relationships and experiences into your life.

Perhaps most importantly, self-love sets the tone for how you allow others to treat you. It instills a sense of self-respect that demands the same from those around you. By valuing yourself, you teach others to value you, too. This doesn't mean you won't face rejection or criticism. Still, it means that you'll have the tools to handle it, knowing that the opinions of others don't determine your worth.

Self-love is not just about feeling good in the moment; it's about building a resilient, compassionate, and authentic self that can navigate the complexities of life with grace and strength. It's about recognizing that you are enough, exactly as you are, and that you deserve to be loved, first and foremost, by yourself.

THE MYTHS OF SELF-LOVE

In a world where you're growing and finding your place, self-love is a term you've probably heard over a thousand times. It's praised as the key to happiness, the solution to life's challenges, and the gateway to fulfillment. But as we peel back the layers of what self-love truly means, let's debunk some of the myths that might be holding you back from fully embracing and understanding it.

Loving Yourself Is Selfish

Firstly, there's a common misconception that self-love comes with selfishness. This couldn't be further from the truth. Loving yourself doesn't mean you disregard the feelings or needs of others. It means you recognize your worth, understanding that you can't pour from an empty cup. When you take care of yourself, you're better positioned to care for and empathize with others.

Self-Love Is All About Treating Yourself

Another myth is that self-love is all about pampering yourself with material things or experiences. While treating yourself can be a part of self-care, self-love is much deeper than that. It's about the internal conversations you have with yourself, the ability to forgive yourself for mistakes, and the commitment to support your growth and happiness. It's not just about feeling good in the moment but having respect towards yourself that carries you through life's ups and downs.

Self-Love Is a Destination

There's also a belief that self-love is a destination—a point you reach where you're entirely content and free from self-doubt or criticism. The truth is that self-love is a journey, not a fixed state. It's normal to have days when you don't love yourself. What matters is the ongoing effort to treat yourself compassionately, recognizing that you are a work in progress.

Self-Love Is Conditional

Lastly, the idea that self-love can only be achieved once you've reached certain milestones or look a certain way is a myth. Your worth is not dependent on your achievements, appearance, or any external factors. Self-love starts from within, from an acceptance of who you are at this moment.

By debunking these myths, we pave the way for a more genuine and empowering understanding of self-love. It's not about perfection or external validation but about embracing your unique journey, with all its imperfections, and treating yourself with the same kindness you'd offer to someone you love deeply.

Let's now explore how to lay the groundwork for deep self-love, setting the stage for growth, resilience, and a happier life.

HOW TO LET YOUR SELF-LOVE GROW

Understanding and debunking the myths that surround self-love is just the beginning. Now, we pivot towards laying down the foundation upon which your self-love can grow and flourish. This foundation is not made from the external validations or achievements that society often tells us to chase. Instead, it is built from the inside out, starting with the core of who you are.

Self-Awareness

Let's begin with self-awareness. Self-awareness goes hand-in-hand with self-love. It involves taking a deep, honest look at yourself — your thoughts, feelings, motivations, and behaviors. It's about recognizing your strengths and accepting your weaknesses without judgment. This process isn't always easy. It requires courage to face yourself and acknowledge the parts of you that you might wish to change.

Self-Compassion

Once you've started practicing self-awareness, the next step is to practice self-compassion. Imagine speaking to yourself as you would to a close friend. You wouldn't criticize a friend for making a mistake or not being perfect, so why do it to yourself? Self-compassion means being kind and understanding when you fail or confront your personal flaws. Imperfection is part of the human experience, and everyone experiences it at some point in their lives.

Setting Boundaries

Setting boundaries is another crucial element of your foundation. Boundaries help protect your energy and emotional well-being. They are the guidelines you set for how you want to be treated by others and how you treat yourself. This might mean learning to say no, prioritizing your needs, or distancing yourself from toxic relationships. We will explore boundaries in more detail in later chapters.

Gratitude

Lastly, gratitude plays a significant role in the building of self-love. Gratitude shifts your focus from what you are missing to what is already in your life. It's about appreciating the small victories, the beauty in the every day, and the lessons learned from challenges. By practicing gratitude, you encourage a positive mindset that supports growth and self-love. We'll explore gratitude in more detail later on in the book.

Building a strong foundation for self-love is an ongoing process. It doesn't happen overnight, and there will be setbacks. But with each step you take — through self-awareness, self-compassion, setting boundaries, and practicing gratitude — you are laying down the stones on your path toward a deeper, more fulfilling relationship with yourself. This is your journey, unique and beautiful, and it's all about becoming the best version of yourself, one step at a time.

CHAPTER SUMMARY

- Self-love is a journey of discovery, growth, and acceptance that is important for one's personal well-being and fulfillment.
- Self-love involves embracing all aspects of yourself, including your strengths, weaknesses, successes, and setbacks, and recognizing your worth.
- The journey of self-love involves learning to be your own best friend, setting boundaries that honor well-being, and making choices that reflect self-love.
- Self-love is important for teenage girls, as it builds a sense of self-worth and confidence, especially during their adolescent years, which are filled with challenges and pressures.
- Several myths about self-love include the misconceptions that self-love is selfish, materialistic, a fixed destination, or depending on your achievements or appearance.
- Self-awareness, self-compassion, setting boundaries, and practicing gratitude can help lay the foundation for growth in self-love, emphasizing the process and journey over perfection.

CHAPTER 1
DISCOVERING WHO YOU ARE

One of the most exciting paths in the journey of discovering who you are is exploring your unique self. This exploration is not about fitting into predefined molds or meeting society's expectations. It's about uncovering who you really are—your passions, quirks, strengths, and even your struggles. It's about embracing every part of yourself with love and compassion.

Your uniqueness is your superpower. It's what sets you apart from everyone else in the world. Think about it—out of billions of people, there is only one you. You have a combination of talents, thoughts, feelings, and experiences that nobody else has. This uniqueness is not something to shy away from; it's something to celebrate!

To start embracing your unique self, acknowledge and accept your feelings and thoughts as valid. It's okay to feel deeply, have opinions, and see the world differently. Your perspective adds valuable color to the canvas of life.

Consider your strengths and weaknesses honestly. Everyone has both, and recognizing them is not about judging yourself but about getting to know yourself better. Your strengths are your gifts to the world, while your weaknesses are opportunities to learn and improve.

Your understanding of yourself will change as you grow. Be patient and kind to yourself through this process. Celebrate your wins, learn from your setbacks, and always remember you are in charge of self-love.

By celebrating your unique self, you're supporting your well-being and setting a powerful example for others. You're showing the world that it's okay to be different, follow your own path, and love yourself every step of the way.

In the next section, we'll delve deeper into what shapes us—our values and beliefs. These guiding principles influence our thoughts, decisions, and actions. Understanding your values and beliefs is crucial for living authentically and fostering a true sense of self-love.

YOUR VALUES AND BELIEFS

Understanding your values and beliefs is like uncovering the compass that guides your heart and soul. These silent whispers steer you through life's many paths, helping you decide what feels right and doesn't align with your life.

Values and beliefs are the colors with which you paint your world. They influence your decisions, shape your dreams, and mold your reactions to the world around you. They are deeply personal, often inherited from the people you love, and uniquely yours to embrace or question as you grow older.

Imagine your values as seeds planted within you. With proper care, these seeds grow into strong trees that provide shelter and direction throughout your life. These values might include honesty, loyalty, and self-compassion—qualities that resonate with who you want to be.

On the other hand, beliefs are the narratives we hold about the world, ourselves, and our place within it. They can be empowering, telling us we are capable and deserving of love, or limiting, holding us back with doubts and fears. We must examine these beliefs and ask ourselves if they truly serve us or need to be gently released.

Discovering your values and beliefs takes time and effort. It's a journey that involves turning inward, being curious, and sometimes, having the courage to challenge what you've always thought to be true. It's about asking yourself the hard questions: What matters most to me? Why do I believe what I believe? How do these beliefs shape my view of myself and the world?

Your values and beliefs are allowed to evolve. As you grow and change, so too can your understanding of what matters most. This is not a sign of inconsistency but of growth. Embrace this evolution because it shows your commitment to becoming the most authentic version of yourself.

When you embrace your values and beliefs, you can live a life with more purpose and passion. You can navigate life's challenges gracefully and confidently. You learn to make choices that align with your deepest truths, leading to a sense of inner peace.

Your values and beliefs are the roots from which your strengths and talents blossom. They shape not just the person you are today but the incredible person you are becoming. Welcome this journey of discovery, because when you understand your values and beliefs, you unlock the full potential of your unique, beautiful self.

YOUR STRENGTHS AND TALENTS

Recognizing and embracing your strengths and talents is like uncovering hidden treasures within yourself. Each of us is a unique blend of abilities and gifts, and finding what you naturally excel at is empowering and a fundamental step toward building self-love.

Think of your strengths as your personal superpowers. These could range from being a good listener, having a knack for solving puzzles, and expressing yourself creatively through art, music, or writing.

Your talents, on the other hand, are the skills you've practiced or are naturally good at. You may have a green thumb, a gift for storytelling, or an exceptional ability in sports. These strengths and talents contribute to who you are, and acknowledging them helps you appreciate your uniqueness.

Discovering your strengths and talents might require some reflection. Start by reflecting on activities that bring you joy or tasks you find fulfilling. Often, our strengths are intertwined with our passions. Ask yourself, what are the things you do that make time fly? What are the tasks that people often come to you for help with? The answers to these questions are clues to your inherent strengths and talents.

It's also beneficial to seek feedback from those who know you well. Sometimes, others can see the brilliance in us that we might overlook. Friends, family members, and teachers can offer insights into your abilities and talents. However, remember, the aim is not to compare yourself with others but to understand and celebrate your skills.

Once you've identified your strengths and talents, the next step is to develop them. This could mean taking up new hobbies, joining clubs or teams that align with your interests, or simply dedicating time to practice and improve. Embracing and developing your talents boosts your self-esteem and opens up opportunities for personal growth and satisfaction.

Your strengths and talents are a significant part of what makes you unique. They are tools for achieving success and ways to find joy and purpose in life.

As you continue to explore and understand yourself, remember that your quirks are also integral to your identity. They add depth to your character and make you who you are. Embracing these aspects of yourself is as important as recognizing your strengths and talents.

EMBRACING YOUR QUIRKS

After thinking about your strengths and talents, it's time to turn our attention to something equally important and delightful—your quirks. These are the unique traits and habits that make you, well, you. They might be the things you've been teased about, or perhaps you've tried to hide them, thinking they make you stand out too much. But here's a secret: those very quirks make you unforgettable and irreplaceably you.

Embracing your quirks is like giving yourself a big, warm hug. It acknowledges that even the parts of you that don't fit into typical boxes are worthy of love and celebration. Think about the people you admire most; aren't their quirks what make them stand out? The way they laugh, the passions they pursue, or even the unique way they see the world—these are the things that draw us to them.

Your quirks could be anything from a passion for collecting something unusual to an eccentric fashion sense, a unique way of expressing yourself, or even an uncommon hobby. Whatever it is, it reflects your inner world, creativity, and perspective on life. Embracing these aspects of yourself can be a powerful step toward loving who you are.

But how do you start embracing these quirks, especially if you've spent years trying to cover them up? Begin by acknowledging them. Write them down, talk about them, or express them in any way you can. Then, try to understand why you felt the need to hide them. Often, it's because we fear judgment or rejection. But remember, anyone who doesn't appreciate the real you isn't someone whose opinion should matter to you.

Next, celebrate your quirks. Wear that quirky outfit with pride, dive into your unusual hobbies, and let your unique light shine brightly. The more you do it, the more you'll find people who love and appreciate you for who you truly are—quirks and all. These are the people who matter. These are the connections that will enrich your life.

Some days, you'll feel bold and unapologetic. On other days, you might feel the urge to retreat. That's okay. Self-love and acceptance are practices that take time. As you continue to embrace your quirks, you'll find that they are not just things to be tolerated but celebrated. They are the essence of your individuality, the signature of your soul. And in a world that often tries to fit us into neatly labeled boxes, choosing to love every part of yourself is a radical act of self-love.

So, let's not just dream about a future where we're fully accepted. Let's create it, starting with accepting and loving ourselves, quirks and all.

REALIZING YOUR DREAMS

After embracing your quirks, it's time to delve deeper into the essence of who you are and who you aspire to be. This journey of self-discovery is not just about recognizing your unique traits but also about discovering your dreams. Dreams are sparks for your future, ignited in your imagination and fueled by your hopes and aspirations.

Dreams hold immense power. They are not just fantasies or fleeting thoughts that pass through your mind. They reflect your innermost desires and potential. When you dream, you allow yourself to picture a life beyond your current reality. You open up to the possibilities of achieving greatness, experiencing joy, and impacting the world.

The path to realizing your dreams is not always straightforward. It requires courage, perseverance, and self-belief. There will be moments of doubt and fear when your dreams seem too distant or challenging to achieve. This is where self-love comes into play. Loving yourself means believing in your ability to overcome obstacles and reach for the stars, even when others might doubt you.

To harness the power of your dreams, start by permitting yourself to dream big. Allow your imagination to run wild without criticism or judgment. Write down your dreams, no matter how grand or silly they may seem. Visualizing your dreams can make them more concrete and achievable.

Next, take actionable steps toward your dreams. Break them down into smaller, manageable goals. Celebrate each progression, no matter how small, as it brings you one step closer to your dream. Remember, the journey toward your dreams is as important as the destination. It is a journey of growth, learning, and self-discovery.

Surround yourself with positivity and support. Seek mentors and role models who inspire and believe in your potential. Their guidance and encouragement can be invaluable as you navigate the challenges and setbacks that may arise.

Lastly, never lose sight of the essence of who you are. Your dreams are a reflection of your unique spirit and potential. Embrace them with open arms and a loving heart. Believe in yourself and your ability to make your dreams a reality. The power of dreams is limitless, and so is your potential to achieve them.

CHAPTER SUMMARY

- Discovering your unique self involves embracing your passions, quirks, strengths, and weaknesses and celebrating what sets you apart.

- Acknowledging and accepting your feelings and thoughts as valid is important in embracing your uniqueness.
- Exploring your interests and what you love doing can provide clues to your passions, contributing to your unique identity.
- Recognizing your strengths and weaknesses allows for personal growth and a better understanding of yourself.
- Embracing your unique self is a lifelong journey that involves patience, self-love, and acceptance, setting a powerful example for others.
- Understanding and aligning with your values and beliefs is essential for living authentically and fostering self-love.
- Recognizing and nurturing your strengths and talents is fundamental to building self-esteem and discovering joy and purpose in life.
- Embracing your quirks and allowing yourself to dream big are vital steps in the journey of self-discovery, leading to a more fulfilling and authentic life.

CHAPTER 2
CULTIVATING POSITIVE SELF-TALK

One of the most powerful tools you can have in your toolkit is self-talk. This continuous stream of thoughts can be your greatest friend or your most formidable foe, depending on its nature. Understanding self-talk is important because it shapes how you view yourself and the world around you. Self-talk influences your confidence, decisions, and, ultimately, the path your life takes.

Self-talk is the inner voice that narrates your day-to-day experiences. It comments on your performance, how you look and interact with others, and much more. This voice can be kind and encouraging, or it can be critical, demeaning, and negative. The nature of your self-talk plays a big role in your mental and emotional well-being.

For many teen girls, the inner critic can be particularly loud. It might tell you that you're not good enough, smart enough, or pretty enough. These messages can hurt your self-esteem and reduce your ability to see your true worth.

The good news is that self-talk is a habit, and like any habit, it can be changed. The first step in transforming self-talk is to listen to your thoughts. Pay attention to the times when your inner voice is more critical than supportive. What triggers these thoughts? Are they tied to specific events, people, or feelings of inadequacy?

Once you start noticing patterns in your self-talk, you can question its credibility. Often, you'll find that these harsh judgments are not based on facts but rather on fears, insecurities, or past experiences that no longer serve you. Recognizing this is pivotal because it allows you to challenge and change these thought patterns.

Transforming negative self-talk into positive affirmations is not an overnight process. It requires patience, practice, and persistence. Start by gently correcting your inner critic. For instance, if you catch yourself thinking, "I'm not smart enough to ace this test," counter that thought with, "I have studied hard, and I am prepared. I can do this." Over time, these positive affirmations will become your new habit, slowly silencing the critic and empowering your inner cheerleader.

The goal is not to always have a positive inner voice—that's unrealistic. The aim is to have a more supportive inner voice that encourages you to do your best and bounce back from challenges. By transforming your self-talk, you're not just changing how you talk to yourself; you're changing how you live your life, filling it with more love and positivity.

HOW TO CHALLENGE NEGATIVE THOUGHTS

Another empowering step you can take is to challenge negative thoughts when they appear in your mind. If left unchecked, these thoughts can prevent you from recognizing your true potential. It's like having an internal critic who's always ready to point out your flaws, real or imagined. But here's a secret: you have the power to challenge and change this narrative.

First, start to notice when negative thoughts take hold of you. These thoughts may seem like truths but are twisted versions of our fears and insecurities. Recognizing these thoughts for what they are—distortions—is the first step in challenging them.

Once you've identified a negative thought, pause and ask yourself, "Is this really true?" More often than not, you'll find that these thoughts are based on feelings rather than facts. For instance, failing at a task doesn't mean you're a failure; it simply means you're human, and there's room for growth. By questioning your negative thoughts, you start to reduce their power over you.

Another powerful tool for challenging negative thoughts is countering them with evidence from your own life. For every thought that says you can't, remind yourself of the times you did. For every thought that says you're not enough, remember the moments you felt proud of yourself or when others appreciated you. This isn't about creating a false sense of self but balancing the narrative to include your strengths and achievements.

It's also helpful to talk to someone you trust about these thoughts. Sometimes, just voicing these insecurities can lessen their hold on you. A friend, family member, or mentor can offer a different perspective, helping you see yourself more positively.

Lastly, practice compassion towards yourself. Challenging negative thoughts isn't about being harsh or critical; it's about gently guiding yourself toward a more loving and accepting viewpoint. Imagine what you would say to a friend in a similar situation and offer encouragement to yourself. This act of self-compassion is a powerful antidote to negative thoughts.

As you continue to challenge and change the way you talk to yourself, the voice of your internal critic will become less daunting. This process requires patience and practice, and people work on it even as they pass their teenage years.

THE POWER OF AFFIRMATIONS

Another transformative practice you can adopt in the pursuit of self-love is the art of positive affirmations. These powerful statements are not just words; they are declarations of your worth, your capabilities, and your dreams. They can transform your inner dialogue from doubt to empowerment.

Affirmations are based on the principle that our thoughts shape our reality. When you repeatedly affirm your strengths and values, you shift your mindset, focusing on your potential rather than your limitations. This shift doesn't happen overnight, but with consistency, affirmations can rewire your brain to naturally think more positively.

To start, choose affirmations that you can relate to. They

should be statements that spark a light within you, even if a part of you doubts their truth. These statements should be in the present tense, as if they are already true, to help your mind accept them as your current reality. Here are some powerful starting points:

I am worthy of love and respect.

My feelings are valid and I honor my emotional needs.

I have the strength to overcome challenges and grow from them.

Doing my best is enough.

My potential is limitless and I can achieve my dreams.

I embrace my uniqueness and celebrate my individuality.

I am a powerful force of kindness and positivity in the world.

Incorporating affirmations into your day can be simple. You might repeat them in the mirror each morning, write them in your journal, or set reminders on your phone to affirm your worth throughout the day. The key is to engage with these affirmations regularly and with intention.

Affirmations help you approach the challenges you face in life with a mindset that empowers you to believe in yourself. They empower to navigate through them with positivity and confidence. Affirmations remind you of your inner strength and the incredible potential within you.

As you continue practicing affirmations, you'll notice a shift in how you view yourself and the world around you. This shift towards a positive mindset is crucial in your self-love journey.

HOW TO CREATE A POSITIVE MINDSET

What follows from positive affirmations is cultivating a positive mindset. This is not about ignoring the complexities and challenges of life but about choosing to focus on the light, even in darkness. It's about having an attitude that uplifts and supports you, especially when you encounter turbulence and self-doubt.

Creating a positive mindset begins with understanding that your thoughts have power. They can shape your reality, influence your emotions, and even affect your actions. Therefore, it's crucial to become mindful of the narrative that plays in your mind. Are your thoughts serving you, or are they your own harshest critic? The goal here is not to achieve perfection but to lean towards kindness and encouragement within your internal dialogue.

You could use some of the tools from earlier in this chapter to help you do this. For example, one effective way to shift towards a more positive mindset is to challenge negative thoughts when they arise. This doesn't mean you have to fight with every negative thought or judge yourself for having them. Instead, acknowledge them and gently guide your mind towards a more positive or realistic perspective. For instance, if you think, "I can't do anything right," pause and ask yourself, "Is this true?" Challenge this thought with evidence of your successes, no matter how small they may seem.

Another way to foster a positive mindset is to surround yourself with positivity. This includes the people you spend time with, the content you consume on social media, and even the environment you create for yourself. Seek out friendships and communities that uplift you and make you feel good about yourself. Fill your social media feed with accounts that inspire and motivate you rather than those that make you feel inadequate. Create a personal space where you can feel safe and happy.

There will be days when doing this feels effortless and others when it feels like an uphill battle. On those challenging days, remind yourself of your worth and the progress you've made.

As you continue to develop a positive mindset, you'll find that it enhances your relationship with yourself and the world around you. It becomes easier to find joy in the little things, bounce back from setbacks, and pursue your dreams. The light that shines from within you can illuminate the darkest of paths and guide you towards a life filled with self-love and happiness.

THE POWER OF GRATITUDE

Gratitude is a simple yet profound way to shift your focus from what's missing to the abundance of good things around you. Gratitude means valuing the little things in life, finding beauty in what you have, and seeing the value in challenges that make us stronger.

To start practicing gratitude, consider keeping a gratitude journal. Before you sleep, write down three things you're grateful for each night. These don't have to be big events; they can be as simple as a warm cup of tea on a cold morning, a compliment from a friend, or the comfort of your bed at the end of a long day. The act of writing them down shifts your focus and helps you see the positive aspects of your life more clearly.

Another way you can do this is to express gratitude towards others. This can be through a thank you note, a kind message, or a small act of kindness. Expressing gratitude not only brightens someone else's day but also reinforces your own feelings of thankfulness. It can also strengthen your relationships with others.

Gratitude can also be practiced through mindfulness and meditation. Taking a few moments each day to silently acknowledge what you're thankful for can create a sense of peace and contentment.

Here are some examples of things you could be grateful for today:

> I am grateful for my friends who always know how to make me smile.

> I am thankful for my family who always has my back and gives me advice, even when I don't want to hear it.

> I am grateful for the chance to go to school and learn new things.

> I am grateful for my body, which allows me to live my life each day.

> I am thankful for my hobbies because let me express myself and unwind.

> I am thankful for every mistake I've made because each one has taught me something important and made me stronger.

> I am grateful for technology and all the resources I have access to because they connect me to a world of possibilities.

Practicing gratitude doesn't mean ignoring the difficulties in life. It's about finding a balance and acknowledging and appreciating the good alongside the bad. Gratitude can help you have a more positive outlook on life, improve your mental health, and increase your resilience.

By incorporating gratitude into your daily routine, you're taking a significant step towards enabling positive self-talk and having a more loving relationship with yourself. Gratitude is a gentle reminder that, in every moment, there is something to be thankful for. It's within this space of thankfulness that self-love flourishes.

CASE STUDY: LILY'S TRANSFORMATION THROUGH POSITIVE SELF-TALK AND GRATITUDE

As a 17-year-old high school senior, Lily constantly battled her inner critic. Despite her achievements, she struggled with feelings of inadequacy and self-doubt, often comparing herself unfavorably to her peers. This negative self-talk affected her confidence, relationships, and overall outlook on life.

One day, after a particularly disheartening encounter with her inner critic, Lily confided in her school counselor, Maya, who was known for her positive outlook on life. Maya listened with empathy before sharing her own journey of overcoming negative self-talk through the practices of positive affirmations and gratitude.

Inspired by her conversation with Maya, Lily embarked on her journey towards positive self-talk. She became more aware of her inner dialogue, especially when stressed or disappointed. Lily noticed that her inner critic was loudest when she faced challenges or made mistakes, often telling her she wasn't good enough or that she would never succeed.

Determined to change this mindset, Lily started challenging her negative thoughts. Whenever she caught herself being self-critical, she would pause and ask, "Why am I telling myself this?" She then countered these thoughts with proof of her capabilities and past successes, reminding herself what she was good at.

Lily also embraced the power of positive affirmations. Although they sounded silly to her at first, she would stand in front of her mirror each morning and affirm her worth, abilities, and potential. Phrases like "I am capable of achieving my goals," "I am worthy of love," and "I believe in myself" became her daily mantras. These affirmations slowly began to shift her mindset, replacing self-doubt with self-confidence.

Lily started keeping a gratitude journal to complement her positive self-talk practice. Every night before bed, she would write down something she was grateful for that day. Doing this helped Lily focus on the positive aspects of her life, from the support of her friends and family to the more minor things she appreciated in life. Expressing gratitude allowed her to see her struggles as chances to grow rather than as evidence of failure.

Lily's transformation didn't happen overnight, but with patience and persistence, she noticed a significant shift in her outlook on life. Her inner critic became less dominant, replaced by a supportive inner voice encouraging her to pursue her dreams and embrace her imperfections.

Through positive self-talk and gratitude, Lily learned to appreciate herself more and recognize her worth and potential. She discovered that changing how she talked to herself could change how she viewed her life, filling it with more love, joy, and fulfillment.

Lily's story shows the power of positive self-talk and gratitude and how it can transform your relationship with yourself.

CHAPTER SUMMARY

- Self-talk is the internal dialogue that influences your perception, confidence, and life decisions. Self-talk can be either positive or negative.
- Negative self-talk can impact your self-esteem and self-worth, but it's a habit that can be changed.
- Transforming self-talk involves becoming aware of and challenging your negative thoughts and replacing them with positive affirmations.
- Positive affirmations are powerful tools for shifting your mindset towards self-love and empowerment.
- Challenging negative thoughts requires recognizing their distortions, questioning their validity, and countering them with thoughts of your achievements.
- Creating a positive mindset involves mindfulness of your thoughts, challenging negativity, surrounding yourself with positivity, and practicing self-compassion.
- Practicing gratitude, such as keeping a gratitude journal or expressing thankfulness to others, shifts your focus from lack to abundance. Gratitude can enhance your mental health and resilience.
- Cultivating a positive mindset and self-talk, challenging negative thoughts, embracing affirmations, and practicing gratitude are all steps you can take toward embracing self-love.

CHAPTER 3
BUILDING HEALTHY RELATIONSHIPS

Healthy relationships can bring us joy, support, and help us grow. They are like mirrors, showing you not only how others see you but also your true self. Understanding this is especially crucial during your teenage years, a time full of big changes and challenges.

Relationships are all about the connection between individuals. This connection can be created through shared experiences, mutual respect, and understanding. It's about finding those who celebrate you and stand by you when times are tough. These relationships can help us feel like we belong and have a purpose.

However, not all relationships may serve our best interests. Some might stop us from growing or lead us away from the path of self-love. Being able to tell the difference is vital. It's important to learn how to spot relationships that are harmful or exhausting. This means paying attention to your gut feelings and noticing how you feel after spending time with different people. Do they uplift you, or leave you feeling tired and down? Answering these questions can help you choose who to let into your inner circle.

Healthy relationships are reciprocal. They are built on give-and-take, where both people contribute to each other's well-being. This ensures that the relationship is balanced and everyone feels valued and heard. It's about supporting each other's dreams and aspirations while also respecting each other's individuality.

Communication is key in helping these relationships grow. It's through open and honest communication that misunderstandings are cleared, and bonds are strengthened. Learning to express your thoughts and feelings respectfully and listen to others with an open heart will serve you well, not just in personal relationships but in all areas of life.

Remember that the relationships you invest in can impact your life in many ways. They can be a source of comfort, inspiration, and empowerment, helping you become the best version of yourself. So choose wisely and don't be afraid to make new connections.

UNDERSTANDING BOUNDARIES AND RESPECT

Understanding and establishing boundaries is a cornerstone of building healthy relationships. Boundaries are not walls meant to keep people out but rather guidelines that help us communicate our needs, respect ourselves, and gain respect from others. They are essential in all relationships, whether with friends, family, or romantic partners.

Imagine boundaries as invisible lines that help everyone understand what is acceptable and what is not. It's about knowing and expressing your limits comfortably and confidently. For example, if you feel overwhelmed by too much social interaction, it's okay to say, "I need some quiet time to recharge." This simple act of setting a boundary honors your need for space and teaches others how to treat you with the respect you deserve.

Respect, much like boundaries, is a two-way street. It involves listening to and honoring the boundaries of others just as much as asserting your own. When someone shares their boundaries with you, it shows they trust you. Respecting these limits strengthens the bond between you and the other person, creating mutual respect and understanding.

Setting boundaries and ensuring others respect them can be challenging. Know that saying no does not make you selfish or unkind. It means you are practicing self-respect and self-care, which are essential aspects of self-love.

It's also important to recognize that boundaries can change. Your needs might shift as you grow and evolve, and that's perfectly normal. Checking in with yourself and reassessing your boundaries is a healthy practice. Communicate these changes clearly and kindly to those around you, allowing your relationships to grow and adapt with you. We'll return to boundaries and how to set healthy ones in a later chapter.

Boundaries are especially important in friendships, which we will explore in the next section. Friendships are a vital part of our social lives and personal development. They can bring us support, joy, and companionship, but also need care and attention to flourish. By practicing setting and respecting boundaries, you lay the groundwork for meaningful and lasting connections with your friends.

HOW TO NAVIGATE FRIENDSHIPS

Navigating friendships during your teenage years can feel like sailing through uncharted waters. There are moments of smooth sailing, unexpected storms, and discoveries of beautiful islands that make the journey worthwhile. This section will help you steer through these waters with grace and confidence.

Friendships are one of life's greatest treasures. They can make us feel happy and supported and positively impact our well-being. However, not all friendships are created equal, and as you grow, your friendships will evolve, too. It's important to recognize that change, including your relationships with friends, is a natural part of life.

Making friends requires patience, care, and finding the right environment. It's about discovering shared interests or experiences, which can help friendships bloom. Be yourself because authenticity attracts genuine connections. Join clubs, sports, or groups that align with your interests, creating opportunities for friendships to form. Remember, a smile, kind words, or even something simple as saying hello can lead to a budding friendship. And just like in life, not every attempt will lead to a friendship, but with time and care, beautiful friendships can flourish, adding vibrant colors to your life.

Understand that it's okay to outgrow friendships. People change, and sometimes, the things you have in common with someone no longer align with who you are or want to be. This doesn't mean you have to completely cut ties or have a dramatic breakup. It simply means permitting yourself to move on, making room for new connections that better match your current self.

Make friends with people who make you feel good about yourself. True friends uplift you and support your dreams. They are the ones who celebrate your successes without jealousy and stand by you when times get tough. These friendships are built on respect, trust, and love for each other. When you find these special friends, make an effort to see them and stay connected. You'll never know; you may still be friends 20 years later!

Friendship is about quality, not quantity. Having a few close friends who truly understand and care for you is more valuable than having a large group of acquaintances.

Friendships are not restricted by age, gender, or location. You might find it easiest to become friends with people in your class or who are the same age as you. But be open to making friends with people from other walks of life. You may meet them through extracurricular activities, shared hobbies, or mutual friends.

As we explored earlier, communication is vital in maintaining healthy friendships. Be open and honest about your feelings, and be a good listener. Friendships thrive when you share and care about each other equally. If you find yourself constantly being the one giving and never receiving, it might be time to reassess that friendship.

Lastly, be yourself. The best friendships are those where you can be your true self, quirks and all, without fear of being judged or teased. These are the friendships that will stand the test of time.

Navigating friendships isn't easy in your teens. It's easy to get swept up by the crowd and want to be friends with the most popular, prettiest, or trendiest people in your school. But it may not be worth your time if these people aren't good friends and don't bring out the best in you.

Friendship requires following your gut, expressing your feelings, and respecting yourself. By understanding your worth and finding the people who recognize and celebrate it, you'll build a network of friendships that will support and enrich your life beyond your teenage years.

Every friendship teaches you something valuable about love, life, and the person you are becoming. Embrace these lessons with an open heart, and you'll find that navigating friendships isn't just about avoiding the storms but also about enjoying the voyage and the companions you meet along the way.

HOW TO DEAL WITH CONFLICT

Conflict will inevitably occur in your relationships. It's a natural part of human interaction, and dealing with these moments can strengthen or weaken our connections with others. As you navigate the ups and downs of teenage life, knowing how to deal with conflict is essential. This section will guide you through these challenging waters to help you emerge stronger and more self-aware.

Conflict, while uncomfortable, is not always bad. It's an opportunity for growth and deeper connection. When a disagreement arises, it's a sign that something needs attention. It could be a boundary being crossed, a need not being met, or a misunderstanding that needs to be clarified. By framing conflict this way, you can approach it with curiosity rather than fear.

Communication is the key to resolving conflict. However, effective communication is more than just talking; it's about listening, understanding, and expressing yourself with clarity and compassion. Start by listening to the other person's perspective without interrupting. This doesn't mean you agree with them, but it shows respect for their feelings and thoughts. When it's your turn to speak, use "I" statements to express your feelings and needs. For example, instead of saying, "You never listen to me," try, "I feel hurt when I don't feel heard." This approach makes you sound less defensive and opens the door to a more productive conversation.

Learn how to recognize and manage your emotions during a conflict. Emotions can run high, and it's easy to react impulsively when you're hurt or angry. However, taking a moment to breathe and calm yourself can significantly affect the outcome. Taking a break from the conversation is okay if you feel overwhelmed. Sometimes, a little space can provide the clarity you need to approach the situation constructively.

Conflict resolution is a skill that requires practice and patience. Not every disagreement will have the outcome you want, and that's okay. What matters is your commitment to treating yourself and others with respect and compassion, even in challenging moments. By embracing conflict as an opportunity for growth, you're building stronger relationships and a deeper sense of self-love.

Your relationship with yourself sets the tone for every other relationship in your life. Embracing self-love in relationships means honoring your feelings, setting healthy boundaries, and treating yourself with the same compassion and respect you offer to others. Self-love empowers you to navigate the complexities of relationships confidently, ensuring that you build truly enriching and supportive connections. Let's explore this more in the next section.

SELF-LOVE IN RELATIONSHIPS

As we navigate through the complexities of teenage years, the relationships we form play an important role in shaping our self-perception and how we engage with the world around us. Self-love guides you, keeps you grounded, and ensures you don't lose yourself when connecting with others.

Self-love in relationships is about recognizing your worth and value independently of anyone else's validation or approval. It's about setting boundaries that protect your emotional well-being and making choices that respect and care for yourself. When you love yourself, you are empowered to form more healthy, supportive, and enriching relationships.

One of the most beautiful aspects of self-love is how it transforms how you relate to others. It encourages you to seek connections that uplift and inspire you rather than those that drain you. It teaches you to be compassionate towards yourself and others, leading to more healthy and fulfilling relationships.

Embracing self-love in relationships also means being brave enough to walk away from situations that harm you. It's about knowing that you deserve to be treated well and refusing to settle for anything less. This might require difficult conversations and tough decisions, but it's crucial to honoring your worth.

Remember, every experience, whether positive or negative, offers valuable lessons that help you grow and better understand what it means to love and be loved healthily.

Self-love is the key to building and sustaining healthy relationships. It's the shield that protects us, the guide that leads us, and the light that illuminates our path to deeper, more meaningful connections. Remember that the most important relationship you will ever have is with yourself.

CASE STUDY: EMMA'S JOURNEY TO SELF-RESPECT AND HEALTHY FRIENDSHIPS

Emma, a 14-year-old high school student, struggled with the dynamics of her main friendship group. Initially, she felt lucky to be included in what many considered the "popular" group. However, as time passed, Emma felt uncomfortable with how the group treated others and herself. They often made plans without consulting her, dismissed her opinions, and sometimes made fun of her interests in art and literature, labeling them as "boring" or "nerdy."

Emma's discomfort reached a tipping point when her friends pressured her to skip a much-anticipated art workshop to attend a party. She realized that she was sacrificing her interests and values to fit in with a group that didn't respect her boundaries or appreciate her for who she was.

Feeling isolated and conflicted, Emma turned to her older sister, Ava, for advice. Ava listened without judgment and encouraged Emma to reflect on what truly made her happy and to think about whether her current friendships aligned with those values.

Emma decided to make a change. She started by setting a boundary with her friends, choosing to attend the art workshop instead of the party. As expected, her decision was met with ridicule, confirming her feelings that these friendships were not healthy for her.

In the following weeks, Emma began exploring new activities that aligned more closely with her interests. She joined the school's art club and volunteered at a local community center, where she met other teenagers who shared her passion for creativity and literature. Gradually, Emma formed new friendships built on respect, shared interests, and support.

Through this transition, Emma learned the value of respecting herself and surrounding herself with people who inspired and appreciated her. She discovered true friends celebrate your successes without jealousy and respect your decisions.

Reflecting on her experience, Emma realized that true friendships aren't just about avoiding negative influences but also about embracing the journey of self-discovery and the joy of connecting with like-minded people. Emma's journey wasn't easy, but it taught her that self-love and setting boundaries are crucial for building healthy, fulfilling relationships. Emma's story shows the power of self-respect and the beauty of finding friendships that enrich your life.

CHAPTER SUMMARY

- Relationships are crucial for joy, support, and growth, acting as mirrors for self-reflection, especially during your teenage years.
- Meaningful relationships are based on shared experiences, mutual respect, and understanding. They can help you feel a sense of belonging and purpose.
- Identifying and avoiding toxic relationships hindering your personal growth is important. Instead, focus on relationships that uplift you and support self-love.

- Healthy relationships are built on give-and-take, ensuring everyone feels valued and heard, supporting each other's dreams, and respecting individuality.
- Communication is key in healthy relationships, with open and honest dialogue clearing misunderstandings and strengthening bonds.
- Establishing and respecting boundaries is essential in all relationships, serving as guidelines for communicating needs and fostering respect for each other.
- Navigating friendships involves being open and honest and seeking out those who inspire and support you.
- Self-love in relationships means recognizing your own worth, setting boundaries for emotional well-being, and pursuing healthy, supportive connections.

CHAPTER 4
EMBRACING YOUR BODY

Imagine walking in a garden full of different, beautiful flowers. Each one is special in its own way, but all are equally stunning. Your body is like one of these beautiful flowers in the big garden of people.

Body image is your view of yourself when you look in the

mirror or think about your appearance. It includes what you think about your looks, your feelings about your body's size, shape, and weight, and how you feel and control your body when you move. It's a mix of thoughts, feelings, and perceptions that can change like the ocean's tides.

Self-esteem is how much you value yourself. It is closely connected to self-respect and self-worth. Imagine self-esteem as the soil that nourishes the roots of your personal garden. When the soil is rich and well cared for, the plants that grow are strong and vibrant. In the same way, strong self-esteem helps you maintain a positive view of your body.

Keeping a positive view of your body and self-esteem can be tricky, especially in today's society, where media and social expectations often dictate beauty standards. Comparing yourself to unrealistic ideals and striving for perfection can turn into a struggle with your body image, harming your confidence and self-love.

But here's the empowering truth: your body is incredible in so many ways. It's what carries you through life's adventures. Every scar, every curve, every freckle reflects your uniqueness. Learning to appreciate your body for its strength and capability rather than just its appearance is crucial to fostering a healthy body image and self-esteem.

Overcoming body image issues is a step in your journey toward self-love and acceptance. Start by practicing compassion towards yourself. Surround yourself with positive influences—friends and media that celebrate all body types and encourage self-care over perfection. Remember, your appearance doesn't measure your worth. Focus on what your body can do, not just how it looks. Practice gratitude for your body's capabilities, whether dancing to your favorite song, laughing until your stomach hurts, or simply taking a deep breath. Challenge negative thoughts with gentleness and remind yourself that beauty is diverse and unique, just like you. It's okay to have tough days, but remember, you're more than a reflection in the mirror—you're a wonderful blend of talents, dreams, and experiences.

Self-esteem grows when you challenge and overcome negative thoughts about your body. It's a journey of small steps, of choosing to see the beauty in difference and the strength in individuality.

Just like a garden thrives with a variety of flowers, the world is enriched by the diversity of its people. Embracing and celebrating this diversity is not just an act of self-love but a reminder that beauty comes in all forms.

CELEBRATING DIVERSITY

Each of us is a unique masterpiece, intricately designed with differences that make us who we are. Recognizing and honoring the variety of body shapes, sizes, colors, and abilities in the world around us is essential. This celebration is about acknowledging these differences and learning to see them as a source of strength and beauty.

There is no single standard for beauty. Society often presents a very narrow view of what it means to be attractive, but this perspective doesn't reflect the rich diversity of human life. Your individuality is what makes you uniquely beautiful. By embracing this truth, you can begin to free yourself from comparisons and embrace your beauty with confidence.

Celebrating diversity also means appreciating your body for what it is capable of rather than focusing only on how it looks. Your body allows you to experience the world, express emotions, and engage in activities you love. Recognizing and valuing these abilities can shift your perspective from criticism to gratitude.

Be kind and compassionate towards others and their bodies. Choosing to spread positivity and acceptance can make a big difference in a world where judgment and body shaming are all too common. It's about creating a supportive community where everyone feels valued and respected, regardless of appearance.

BUILDING HEALTHY HABITS

Healthy habits are not just about what you eat or how often you exercise. They help you build a relationship with your body that is kind, forgiving, and supportive. Let's explore how you can form healthy habits in a way that feels empowering and sustainable.

Start by listening to your body's cues and responding with care. This means eating when you're hungry, resting when you're tired, and moving in ways that bring you joy. It's not about strict diets or rigorous exercise routines; it's about balance and finding what makes your body feel good.

Incorporate a variety of foods into your diet that nourish your body and soul. There's no need to label foods as "good" or "bad." Instead, aim for a colorful plate filled with fruits, vegetables, proteins, and grains you enjoy. Listen to your body's needs and cravings, and fulfill them with a balance of nutrients and treats. Your relationship with food should be one of enjoyment and nourishment, not punishment or guilt. Remember, it's perfectly okay to indulge in your favorite treats. The key is moderation, not deprivation.

Physical activity is also an excellent way to care for your body. Exercise not only improves physical health but also boosts mental well-being. Find a form of movement you genuinely enjoy, whether dancing, yoga, walking with your friends, or playing a team sport. The goal is to move your body in ways that feel joyful and stimulating, not tedious or overwhelming.

Sleep is another crucial healthy habit. Your body needs time to rest and recharge, so aim for 7-9 hours of sleep each night. Create a calming bedtime routine that signals to your body it's time to wind down. This might include reading, gentle stretching, or listening to soothing music. Listen to your body when it signals that it's tired or overwhelmed, and respond with kindness by giving it the rest it deserves.

Lastly, hydration is vital. Drinking enough water each day helps your body function at its best. Carry a water bottle with you as a reminder to drink regularly. If you find water too bland, try adding fruit slices or a splash of juice for a hint of flavor.

Adopting healthy habits is a form of self-love and self-care. It's about making choices that honor your body's needs and improve your well-being. Be patient with yourself as you explore what habits work best for you. It's a process of trial and error, and it's okay to adjust your approach as you learn more about what makes you feel your best.

HOW TO DEAL WITH BODY SHAMING

One of the hurdles you might face during your teenage years is body shaming. It's an unfortunate reality that, at some point, you may encounter negative comments or attitudes about your body from others. These can come from peers, social media, and sometimes, even from family members. It's vital to understand that body shaming is more about the other person's unresolved issues and not a reflection of your worth or beauty.

First and foremost, know that your worth isn't lessened

because someone else might not recognize your value. You are so much more than a body. You are a lively soul with dreams, passions, and the ability to change the world. Your body carries you through this life, and it should be treated with care and love, not negativity.

When faced with body shaming, return to your positive thinking and self-love practices. This means actively appreciating your body for what it can do rather than how it looks. Celebrate the small things, like how your legs carry you through your day or how your arms allow you to hug your loved ones. These may seem simple, but they are profound acts of gratitude towards yourself.

Surround yourself with friends and family who uplift and remind you of your worth. Surround yourself with positivity and limit your exposure to toxic environments or social media accounts that make you feel inadequate. Remember, you can curate your social media feed with accounts that celebrate body diversity and promote self-love.

Be kind to yourself. When negative thoughts about your body arise, challenge them with positive affirmations. Remind yourself that perfection is an unattainable and unnecessary goal. You are perfectly imperfect, and that's what makes you special.

If body shaming is affecting your mental health, don't be afraid to seek support from a trusted adult, counselor, or therapist. Sometimes, having someone else guide you through these feelings can provide the tools you need to navigate them more effectively. You are worthy of love and respect, just as you are. Embrace your body because it is the only one you have and is beautiful.

CASE STUDY: MIA'S PATH TO BODY POSITIVITY AND SELF-LOVE

Mia, a 15-year-old high school sophomore, always felt out of place in her skin. Growing up, she was taller and more muscular than most of her peers, which made her feel self-conscious and, at times, less feminine. Mia's discomfort with her body was compounded by the endless stream of perfect images she saw on social media and the occasional thoughtless comments from classmates and even family members.

One day, during a physical education class, Mia overheard a group of students making fun of her athletic build. The comments hurt her, and she spent the rest of the day trying to shrink herself and appear smaller and less noticeable. That night, Mia shared her feelings with her best friend, Lena.

Lena listened intently before sharing her own journey of coming to love her body. She emphasized the importance of self-compassion and the realization that bodies are meant to be diverse and capable, not just things to look at. Lena introduced Mia to body positivity and showed Mia some inspirational figures she followed on social media who advocate for self-love and body diversity.

Inspired by her conversation with Lena, Mia began to curate her social media feeds, unfollowing accounts that made her feel inadequate and seeking out those that celebrated all body types. She discovered a community of people who celebrated their unique features and spoke openly about the journey to self-acceptance. This was a revelation for Mia, who had never considered that her athletic build could be a source of strength and beauty.

Mia also started to explore activities that made her appreciate her body for what it could do rather than how it looked. She joined the school's track team, where her height and strength became her greatest assets. Running gave Mia a sense of freedom and confidence. She loved the feeling of her muscles powering her forward. She began to see her body as a capable and incredible vessel for her passions.

As Mia's perspective shifted, she found herself more willing to stand up against body shaming, not just directed at her but also at others. She became an advocate for body positivity among her peers, encouraging them to see their own beauty and strength. Mia's journey wasn't without its challenges, but with each step, she grew more confident in her skin.

Mia's transformation also had a ripple effect on her friends and family. Her newfound self-assurance and advocacy for body diversity inspired those around her to reconsider their own views on beauty and self-worth.

Mia learned that self-esteem blooms from within, nurtured by self-respect, kindness, and the celebration of one's capabilities. She discovered that beauty is not a one-size-fits-all concept but a diverse garden where every flower thrives by simply being its unique self. Mia's path to body positivity and self-love was a journey back to herself, recognizing and embracing the beauty of her natural self. Mia's story is a testament to the power of self-love and the importance of celebrating the unique beauty in everyone.

CHAPTER SUMMARY

- Understanding the relationship between body image and self-esteem is essential for embracing your body.

- Body image involves perceptions, feelings, and thoughts about your appearance, which can change over time and be influenced by societal standards.
- Self-esteem is the overall value you place on yourself and can help you maintain a positive body image.
- Today's media and societal beauty standards can make it hard to maintain a positive body image and self-esteem, leading to comparisons and unrealistic expectations.
- Embracing your body and appreciating it for its capabilities is vital to fostering a healthy body image and self-esteem.
- Practicing kindness towards yourself, celebrating your body's abilities, and challenging negative thoughts can help improve self-esteem and body image.
- Celebrating diversity and recognizing the beauty in different body shapes, sizes, and abilities enriches your self-acceptance and contributes to a more inclusive world.
- Developing healthy habits, dealing with body shaming through self-love and support, and practicing self-care are essential for fostering a positive relationship with your body.

CHAPTER 5
FINDING YOUR CREATIVE SIDE

Finding and growing your creative side is a vital part of loving yourself and growing as a person. Being creative isn't just about making art or writing stories; it's about expressing yourself in your unique way. It's about enjoying creating something, no matter the result.

Everyone has a unique creative spark waiting to be ignited. It might be in how you see the world, the ideas that dance through your mind, or the hobbies that make your heart sing. The key is to allow yourself to explore and experiment without judgment or fear of failure. Creativity is not a competition. It's a personal journey of exploration and expression.

To find your creative spark, start by paying attention to the activities that make you lose track of time, the topics that light up your eyes when you talk about them, and the dreams that fill you with excitement. These are clues pointing towards your passions and interests. Allow yourself to follow these clues with curiosity and openness. Try new things, even if they seem daunting at first. You might discover a love for something you never expected.

Another powerful way to ignite your creativity is to create a creativity journal. This journal can be a space where you jot down ideas, sketch, write poems, or insert pictures that inspire you. There's no right or wrong way to use it; the goal is simply to make space for your thoughts and inspirations. Over time, this journal can become a treasure trove of ideas and a reminder of your creative journey.

If you don't know where to start, here are some activities you can try to channel your creative energy:

- Writing poetry or short stories
- Drawing in a sketchbook
- Coloring in or painting
- Creating digital art or graphic design
- Starting a DIY fashion or jewelry project
- Experimenting with photography or videography
- Designing and creating a personal blog or vlog
- Learning to play a musical instrument or write songs

- Exploring different types of dance or choreography
- Crafting handmade gifts or decorations for your room

Don't be afraid to share your creations with others. Sharing can be scary, but it can also be incredibly rewarding. It's a way to connect with others, receive feedback, and grow as a creator. Remember that everyone was once a beginner. What matters most is that you're taking steps to express yourself and bring your unique perspective to the world.

Embracing your creativity will enrich your life and inspire those around you. Your creative spark is a gift; the world is waiting to see what you'll do with it. So explore, create, and let your light shine brightly.

HOW TO OVERCOME CREATIVE BLOCKS

Encountering creative blocks is a natural part of the creative process. While frustrating, these blocks are not barriers but stepping stones toward deeper self-understanding and growth. Embracing your creative blocks with consideration and curiosity can transform them from obstacles to opportunities.

Creative blocks often signal a need for rest or a change of perspective. Your mind is a garden that requires both sunshine and rain; periods of intense creativity must be balanced with rest and replenishment. When you hit a block, it might be your inner self telling you it's time to take a break. Break up your creative time with activities that make you feel happy and relaxed, whether reading, walking outside, or spending time with loved ones. These moments of rest are not a detour from your creative path but an essential part of the process.

Comparison can be the thief of joy and creativity. In a world amplified by social media, it's easy to fall into the trap of comparing yourself to others. Remember, your creativity is as unique as your fingerprint and cannot be compared to anyone else's. When you are caught in the comparison spiral, gently guide your focus back to your own path. Celebrate your creativity and progress, no matter how small it may seem.

You could embrace the power of journaling to unlock your creative blocks. Writing down your thoughts, fears, and dreams can clarify your emotions and ideas, allowing new inspiration. Sometimes, the act of writing can reveal hidden insights and solutions that were buried within you. Allow your journal to be a safe space where your creativity can flow, free from judgment.

Lastly, seek inspiration in the world around you. This could mean spending time in nature, visiting art galleries, reading books, or listening to music that moves you. Explore new hobbies, engage with different art forms, and open yourself to new experiences. Inspiration can be found everywhere, but you must be open to receiving it. Sometimes, the simplest experiences can spark the most profound ideas.

Overcoming creative blocks is not about forcing inspiration but nourishing your creativity with patience and love. Each block invites you to explore deeper aspects of yourself and your passion. By approaching these challenges with openness and positivity, you'll discover that the path beyond the block is richer and more rewarding than you imagined.

HOW TO SET GOALS FOR YOUR PROJECTS

After overcoming creative blocks, it's time to take a step forward by setting goals for your passion projects. This process is not just about achieving outcomes but also about understanding yourself better and appreciating your unique talents.

Setting goals begins with clarity. Ask yourself, "What do I love doing so much that time seems to fly by when I'm doing it?" Whether writing, painting, coding, or anything else that sets your heart on fire, identifying this passion is the first step. Once you know your passions, it's time to dream big. Allow yourself to envision the most magnificent possibilities from your passion. Remember, this is your personal canvas, and you're free to paint it with the colors of your wildest dreams.

Dreams and passions need a structure to thrive, which is where goal setting comes into play. Start by breaking down your big dream into smaller, achievable goals. These should be specific, measurable, attainable, relevant, and time-bound (SMART).

For example, if your dream is to become a writer, a SMART goal could be to write at least 500 words daily or to finish the first draft of a short story within three months. By setting such goals, you're creating a roadmap that will guide you toward your larger vision.

Be flexible with your goal-setting process. Sometimes, the path to our dreams takes unexpected turns, and that's okay. Being open to change and adapting your goals shows strength and self-awareness. Each step you take and goal you achieve brings you closer to finding your passions and, ultimately, yourself.

As you explore your creativity and passions, remember to celebrate every milestone, no matter how small it may seem. Celebrating your achievements is an act of self-love that reinforces your belief in your abilities and boosts your motivation to keep moving forward. Whether it's finishing a sketch, learning a new chord on the guitar, or writing a poem that speaks your truth, every achievement shows your dedication and love for your passion.

Your passion and creativity projects are not just tasks to be completed; they are expressions of your deepest self. They deserve to be pursued with love and enthusiasm and are just as crucial to your well-being as other aspects of your life. In the next section, you'll discover the importance of discipline in bringing your passion projects to life.

THE ROLE OF DISCIPLINE

Discipline is a word that often conjures images of strict schedules and rules, but in the realm of personal growth and self-love, discipline is something far more gentle and empowering.

Think of discipline not as a set of constraints but as a way to guide you toward your goals. It's about honoring your commitments to yourself, dreams, and passions. When you set goals for your passion projects, you take the first step in a dance with discipline. The following steps involve maintaining momentum, staying focused, and navigating the inevitable challenges that arise so you can achieve your goals.

Discipline means creating a physical and mental space where your creativity can flourish. It's about setting aside time regularly, even if it's just a few minutes each day, to dedicate to your passion projects. This consistent effort builds a structure of commitment and progress toward your goals.

It also involves setting boundaries. In a world filled with distractions, discipline helps you say no to things that might divert your attention and energy away from what truly matters to you. This is about making empowered choices that align with your passion and creativity.

Discipline also teaches you resilience. Not every attempt will be a success, and not every day will feel productive. However, the discipline of showing up for yourself and your passions, even on the tough days, builds an invaluable strength. In these moments, you learn the most about yourself and your passions. You discover new ways to overcome obstacles and find that your creativity isn't just about the highs but also about navigating the lows with positivity and determination.

Discipline in the context of self-love and creativity is not about perfection. It's about progress. It's about showing up and committing to yourself again and again. This disciplined approach isn't a straight path; it's a journey with twists and turns. Each step forward shows your love for yourself and dedication to your dreams.

As you continue to weave discipline into your life, you'll find that it becomes less about external factors and more about internal motivation. It becomes a part of your self-love language, a way to honor your creativity, passion, and, most importantly, yourself.

CELEBRATING YOUR ACHIEVEMENTS

Recognizing and celebrating your achievements is as crucial as the discipline and hard work that got you there. This celebration is not just a reward; it's a vital part of fostering your creativity and passion.

When you take the time to celebrate your achievements, you're sending a powerful message to yourself: that you are worthy of praise, your efforts matter, and you are capable of achieving great things. This can boost your self-esteem, increase your motivation, and fuel your desire to pursue your passions with even more vigor.

But how do you celebrate your achievements in a way that truly honors your journey and encourages your creative spirit? First, celebration doesn't always mean a grand gesture. Sometimes, the most meaningful celebrations are the quiet moments of reflection and gratitude for how far you've come.

One way to celebrate is by keeping a journal of your achievements. This can be a place where you record the milestones you've reached and express your feelings and thoughts about your journey. Writing down your achievements helps solidify them in your mind and allows you to look back and see your progress.

Another way to celebrate is by sharing your successes with others. This could mean telling a friend or family member about a goal you've reached or sharing your creative work with a broader audience. Sharing your achievements not only multiplies your joy but also inspires others to pursue their own passions and goals.

Celebrate in a way that feeds your soul and recharges your creative energy. This could be as simple as taking a day off to do something you love or treating yourself to something special. Do something that makes you feel joyful and alive, something that reminds you why you embarked on this journey in the first place.

Celebrating your achievements is not about ego or boasting. It's about honoring your hard work and creative spirit. It encourages you to keep pushing forward, exploring your passions, and embracing your unique path.

CHAPTER SUMMARY

- Discovering your creative spark can be an important part of self-love and personal growth. It is a form of self-expression and helps you find joy in creation.

- Creativity is a personal journey that requires allowing yourself to explore without fear of judgment or failure. It's not just limited to traditional arts.
- To ignite creativity, focus on activities that you find fun and engaging, and surround yourself with inspiration.
- Sharing your creations with others can be rewarding and is a step towards growth and connection. Remember that everyone once started as a beginner.
- Overcoming creative blocks involves recognizing the need for rest, avoiding comparison, journaling thoughts and fears, and seeking inspiration from the world.
- Setting goals for your passion projects requires clarity, dreaming big, and creating a structured plan with specific, achievable goals.
- Discipline is about self-respect, maintaining momentum, setting boundaries, and learning resilience through the ups and downs of the creative process.
- Celebrating your achievements and progress, no matter how small, boosts your self-esteem and motivation and is a vital part of the creative journey.

CHAPTER 6
MANAGING STRESS AND ANXIETY

Your teenage years are full of change, growth, and exploration. Stress and anxiety are a natural part of life, even during these years. It's not just about the big exams or the social dynamics; it's also about the internal questions and the process of figuring out who you are and where you fit in this vast world. This period of your life is marked by a quest for independence, together with puberty's physical and emotional changes. It can sometimes feel like riding a rollercoaster without a seatbelt.

Understanding that stress and anxiety are natural responses to the pressures and expectations faced during these years is the first step towards managing them. It's okay to feel overwhelmed by the demands of school, relationships, and future plans. It's okay to feel nervous about fitting in or standing out. These feelings are all part of the human experience, but they don't need to define you.

Stress is your body's reaction to change that requires an adjustment or response. Stress can appear in various ways, including physical symptoms like headaches or fatigue, emotional symptoms like irritability or sadness, and behavioral symptoms like withdrawing from activities or changes in eating habits.

Anxiety, on the other hand, is a feeling of fear, dread, or unease about what's to come. Anxiety might make you feel like you're in a constant state of worry or fear, even about things that might seem small to others. It's important to recognize these signs in yourself as signals that your body and mind are asking for attention and care.

One of the most empowering things you can do for yourself is to learn how to navigate these feelings. This doesn't mean pushing them away or pretending they don't exist. Instead, it's about acknowledging them, understanding their cause, and finding healthy ways to manage them. Whether it's through talking to someone you trust, writing down your thoughts, or doing things that bring you joy and relaxation, there are countless ways to support yourself through these feelings.

You are not alone in feeling stress or anxiety. These feelings don't have to be your enemies; they can be your teachers, guiding you toward a better understanding of yourself and your needs. By facing them with compassion, you're taking a significant step on your path to self-love and resilience.

MINDFULNESS AND RELAXATION TECHNIQUES

Mindfulness and relaxation techniques can help guide you through stressful or anxious moments. They can help you feel more at peace and discover your inner strength.

Practicing Mindfulness

Mindfulness is about being fully present in the moment and engaging with your experiences and feelings without judgment. It's like stepping back and observing your thoughts and feelings like leaves floating down a river. You notice and acknowledge them but don't have to pick them up.

You can start practicing mindfulness by dedicating a few minutes each day to simply breathe and be. Sit in a quiet space, close your eyes, and focus on your breath. Inhale deeply, feeling your chest and belly rise, and exhale slowly, feeling a sense of release. Whenever your mind wanders, gently bring your focus back to your breath. This simple act can be incredibly powerful and can help reduce feelings of anxiety.

Progressive Muscle Relaxation

Another powerful technique is progressive muscle relaxation. This involves tensing each muscle group in your body tightly, but not to the point of strain, and then slowly relaxing them. Start from your toes and work your way up to your head. With each tension and release, imagine the stress melting away from your body. This method not only helps with reducing anxiety but also promotes a deeper awareness of your physical self.

Visualization

Visualization is another tool you can add to your self-love toolkit. It involves picturing a place where you feel completely at ease. This could be a real place you've visited or a landscape you created in your mind. Focus on the details—the sounds, the smells, the colors. Feel the peace or happiness that this place brings you. This technique can be a powerful way to shift your focus away from stress and towards a sense of calm.

Journaling

Journaling is also a form of mindfulness that can help you understand and manage your emotions. It's a space where you can express yourself freely without fear of judgment. Write about what you're feeling, why you might be feeling this way, and anything else that comes to mind. Sometimes, the mere act of putting your thoughts on paper can provide relief and help clarify what you're feeling.

Incorporating these mindfulness and relaxation techniques into your daily routine can be transformative. They are not just practices for managing stress and anxiety but are also acts of self-care. By taking the time to nurture your mind and body, you're sending a powerful message to yourself—that you are worthy of care and attention.

THE IMPORTANCE OF SELF-CARE

One of the best things you can do to improve your mental well-being is to practice self-care. Self-care is not just about pampering yourself, though that can be a part of it. It's about caring for your body and listening to what it needs. It's about setting aside time to attend to your well-being, no matter how brief. This section will guide you through the various ways you can practice self-care.

Self-care is about looking after your mental, emotional, and physical well-being. It can be as simple as setting aside time for activities that make you feel happy and relaxed, such as reading a book, taking a long bath, or spending time in nature.

Self-care is also about listening to your body and mind. It's recognizing when you're pushing yourself too hard or on the brink of burnout, whether in physical activities, social engagements, or academic pressures. It's about understanding that saying 'no' to additional responsibilities isn't a sign of weakness but a profound act of self-respect.

Remember, you can't pour from an empty cup. By caring for yourself, you ensure you have the energy and health to pursue your dreams and support those you love.

Another aspect of self-care is hygiene. Taking care of your body by keeping it clean and groomed is a basic yet profound way of showing love for yourself. Whether it's a refreshing shower, a soothing bath, or a skincare routine, these acts of cleanliness can be incredibly grounding and signal to yourself that you are worth taking care of.

Incorporating self-care into your daily life doesn't have to be overwhelming. Start small. It could be as simple as ensuring you're hydrated, taking a few deep breaths to center yourself during a busy day, or setting aside time each week to engage in an activity that brings you joy. Here are some examples of self-care activities you could incorporate into your routine:

- Writing in a journal to express your thoughts and feelings
- Practicing yoga or meditation for relaxation and mindfulness
- Creating art, like drawing or painting, to channel creativity
- Taking a digital detox day to reduce screen time and recharge
- Listening to your favorite music or podcasts
- Engaging in physical activities, such as dancing, hiking, or playing a sport
- Going for a walk outside on a sunny day
- Spending time with pets can boost your mood and provide companionship
- Trying out new hobbies, like cooking or photography, to discover new passions
- Having a bubble bath at the end of a tiring day

Self-care is deeply personal, and what works for one person may not work for another. Try to explore different practices and find what makes you feel the most happy and connected to your body. This could range from simple daily routines to more elaborate self-care rituals. Stay in tune with yourself and be open to changing your self-care practices as your needs and circumstances change.

When you practice self-care, you're taking care of your body and mind and building a foundation of love and respect for yourself. Self-care is an essential part of managing stress and anxiety.

It's a practice that improves your relationship with yourself and equips you to face life's challenges with resilience. It's also about honoring your body for all it does for you, treating it with the care it deserves, and giving yourself some 'me' time. Self-care is not selfish; it's a necessary and beautiful part of loving and caring for yourself.

HOW TO SET HEALTHY BOUNDARIES

Setting healthy boundaries is another pivotal way to manage stress and anxiety. This practice is about saying no to what you don't want and affirming what you need for your mental, emotional, and physical well-being. It's about understanding and respecting your limits and ensuring others do too.

Imagine your energy as a beautiful garden. Just as a garden needs a fence to protect it from being trampled, you need boundaries to protect your energy. Without these boundaries, it's easy to overextend yourself, leading to stress and anxiety. But with them, you create a safe space for your garden to flourish.

Setting boundaries can start with tuning into your feelings. Notice situations that leave you feeling drained or uncomfortable. These feelings are signals, indicating where you need to set a limit. For example, if you are overwhelmed by too many extracurricular activities, it might be time to limit how many activities you do during the week.

Communicating your boundaries is equally important. It's okay to express your needs respectfully and clearly. You might worry about how others will react, but setting boundaries is fundamental to your well-being. Those who care for you will respect your limits and support you.

Enforcing your boundaries is also crucial. Sometimes, you

might need to remind others or distance yourself from those who consistently disrespect your limits. This isn't easy, but it's necessary for your mental health and self-love journey.

Here are some examples of the types of boundaries you could think about setting in your life.

Digital Communication Boundaries

Setting specific times when you aren't available for texting or social media to ensure you have time for homework, self-care, and rest. For example, "I don't check my phone after 9 PM so I can unwind and get a good night's sleep."

Personal Space Boundaries

Communicating your need for personal space, especially in crowded settings or at home. "I need my own space to relax and recharge. Please knock before entering my room."

Emotional Boundaries

Expressing when you are not in a place to take on someone else's emotional baggage or solve their problems. "I care about you, but I'm feeling overwhelmed myself and can't give you the support you need right now."

Academic Boundaries

Saying no to requests that interfere with your study time or academic goals. "I can't hang out on weeknights because I need to focus on my studies."

Physical Boundaries

Being clear about your comfort level with physical touch, even with friends or family. "I'm not really a hugger. I prefer a high-five or a wave."

Privacy Boundaries

Setting limits on sharing your personal information, both online and in person. "I'm not comfortable sharing that story about myself. Let's talk about something else."

Time Management Boundaries

Prioritizing your time and commitments, and saying no to additional responsibilities when necessary. "I appreciate the offer, but I have too much on my plate right now to commit to another project."

Your boundaries can change, and that's okay. As you grow and your life changes, your needs will too. Regularly reflect on your boundaries to ensure they still serve you well.

By setting and respecting healthy boundaries, you protect your well-being and teach others how to treat you. It empowers you to manage stress and anxiety more effectively, paving the way for a more balanced and fulfilling life.

SEEKING SUPPORT WHEN NEEDED

Seeking support is a brave step. It acknowledges that sometimes, the weight we carry is too heavy to bear alone. This doesn't mean you're not strong enough; it means you're wise enough to understand the power of community and connection.

Seeking support can take many forms, and finding what resonates with you is essential. Sometimes, it's about opening up to a trusted friend or family member. Sharing your feelings and experiences can provide a sense of relief and release. It's like letting someone else help you carry your backpack on a long hike. Remember, those who care about you want to support you, even if they might not always know how. Be open with them about what kind of support you need, whether it's a listening ear, advice, or just their presence.

Professional support is another powerful resource. Counselors, therapists, and mental health professionals are trained to help you navigate your feelings and find strategies to manage stress and anxiety. There's no shame in seeking their help; it's a sign of strength and a step towards healing. These professionals can offer you tools and insights that friends and family might not be able to provide, helping you build resilience and a deeper understanding of yourself.

Support groups can offer an incredibly comforting sense of community. Knowing you're not alone in your feelings and experiences can be validating and empowering. These groups provide a safe space to share and learn from others walking a similar path. They remind us that our struggles are part of the human experience, not a reflection of our capabilities.

Seeking support is an act of self-love. It acknowledges that you deserve to feel better and to live a life not dominated by stress and anxiety. It's a step towards embracing your vulnerability as a strength. By reaching out, you're helping yourself and paving the way for others to do the same. You're showing that it's okay not to be okay and that healing is possible with the right support.

As you navigate the waters of seeking support, be patient and kind to yourself. Finding the right type of help and people to support you can take time. But each step you take, no matter how small, is a step towards a more loving relationship with yourself.

CASE STUDY: ALEX'S JOURNEY THROUGH STRESS AND SELF-DISCOVERY

Alex, a 17-year-old high school junior, found themselves caught in a whirlwind of stress and anxiety. With college applications on the horizon, a demanding part-time job, and a bustling social life, Alex felt like they were constantly running on empty. The pressure to excel academically while maintaining a vibrant social media presence only added to their stress, leaving Alex feeling overwhelmed and disconnected from themselves.

One evening, after a particularly tiring day, Alex broke down during a conversation with their mother, Rita. Rita listened patiently before sharing her own experiences with managing stress during her teenage years. Rita introduced Alex to some mindfulness and relaxation techniques and emphasized the importance of self-care and setting healthy boundaries.

Inspired by Rita's advice, Alex decided to take proactive steps towards managing their stress and anxiety. They began by carving out time each morning to practice mindfulness. Sitting quietly in their room, Alex focused on their breathing, allowing themselves to be present in the moment, acknowledging their thoughts and feelings without judgment.

Journaling became a nightly ritual for Alex. They poured their thoughts, fears, and dreams onto the pages, finding clarity and a sense of release. This self-expression helped Alex understand their emotions more deeply and fostered a compassionate relationship with themselves.

Recognizing the importance of self-care, Alex began to set boundaries, both with themselves and others. They learned to say no to extra shifts at work and to social engagements that felt more draining than fulfilling. Alex communicated their needs to friends and family, who supported their decision to prioritize well-being.

Alex also sought support from a school counselor, who provided a safe space to explore their feelings and offered strategies for managing anxiety. This professional guidance was instrumental in helping Alex navigate their stressors more effectively.

As Alex implemented these changes, they noticed a profound shift in their mental and emotional state. The overwhelming waves of stress and anxiety began to recede, replaced by a sense of calm and self-assuredness. Alex discovered joy in simple pleasures, like reading for leisure and taking walks with their mother, activities that had fallen by the wayside amid their busy schedule.

Alex learned that managing stress and anxiety is not about eliminating challenges but about having a compassionate relationship with oneself. They realized the importance of listening to their body and prioritizing their well-being over academic or extracurricular demands.

Alex's story shows the power of vulnerability and taking steps towards self-discovery and healing. It highlights the importance of acknowledging stress and anxiety as part of the teenage experience and the transformative potential of self-care, mindfulness, and support in navigating this phase of life.

CHAPTER SUMMARY

- Teenage years are particularly prone to stress and anxiety due to changes, growth, and the quest for identity and independence.
- Stress and anxiety are natural responses to changes in life. Ways to manage them include acknowledging these feelings and finding supportive activities.
- Mindfulness and relaxation techniques, such as deep breathing, progressive muscle relaxation, visualization, and journaling, can help manage stress and anxiety.
- Self-care is essential in managing stress and anxiety. It involves recognizing your needs and taking steps to meet them, affirming your own self-worth.
- Setting healthy boundaries is crucial for protecting your mental, emotional, and physical well-being. It involves understanding and respecting personal limits.
- Seeking support, whether through friends, family, professionals, or support groups, is a step you can take to manage stress and anxiety.

CHAPTER 7
THE POWER OF RESILIENCE

R esilience is a word you might have heard quite a bit. But what does it truly mean, especially for you, a vibrant and evolving teen girl? Resilience is the remarkable ability to bounce back from challenges, setbacks, and failures. It's about facing a difficult situation head-on and emerging from it stronger and wiser than before.

Imagine resilience as a muscle in your heart and mind. It gets stronger every time you use it. Like any muscle, it requires practice, time, and care to develop. Life can sometimes throw curveballs your way. These could be anything from a bad grade on a test to a fallout with a friend or any other disappointment that life might present. In these moments, your resilience shines through, helping you navigate these situations with power and positivity.

Resilience is not about constantly feeling happy or never facing difficulties. It's about how you respond to and grow from these experiences. It's about acknowledging your feelings, learning from your mistakes, and moving forward with a positive attitude. This doesn't mean ignoring your emotions or pretending everything is okay when it's not. It's about giving yourself the time and space to feel, heal, learn, and step forward into your next chapter.

You already possess the ability to adapt and thrive. It's woven into your very being, waiting for moments to reveal its strength. And the beauty of resilience? It grows with you. Each challenge you face and overcome adds another layer to your resilience, making you even more capable of handling whatever life throws your way next.

So, whenever you face a new challenge, remember you are resilient. You have within you the power to overcome, learn, and grow.

HOW TO BUILD A RESILIENT MINDSET

Now, let's delve into how you can build a resilient mindset.

Building a resilient mindset isn't about shielding yourself from every hardship or pretending that challenges don't exist. It's about developing inner strength that helps you bounce back from tough experiences, no matter how hard it might seem. This mindset is the invisible armor that protects you, not by making you invulnerable but by empowering you to face life's battles with courage.

Your thoughts and beliefs about yourself play a significant role in resilience. If you constantly tell yourself you're not good enough or can't handle challenges, you're setting yourself up for failure. Instead, try to harness a compassionate inner voice. Speak to yourself with kindness and encouragement. This positive self-talk is a powerful tool in building resilience.

Another key aspect of a resilient mindset is embracing flexibility. Life is unpredictable, and sometimes, despite our best plans and efforts, things don't go our way. Instead of seeing this as a failure, view it as an opportunity to grow. Adaptability is a sign of resilience. It's about finding different paths to your goals and being open to new experiences and perspectives. It's okay to adjust your sails when the wind changes direction.

Resilience is closely tied to problem-solving skills. When faced with a challenge, a resilient person looks for solutions rather than dwelling on the problem. They break down overwhelming situations into manageable parts and tackle them one step at a time. This approach brings a sense of control and accomplishment and builds confidence in your ability to handle future obstacles.

Don't underestimate the power of a support network. Resilience doesn't mean going through tough times alone. It's about knowing when to seek help and lean on the people who care about you. Whether it's family, friends, or mentors, having a circle of support provides emotional strength and a sense of belonging.

Building a resilient mindset is a continuous process. It's about learning from every experience, embracing your vulnerabilities, and recognizing your inner strength. Remember, resilience isn't a trait that some people have and others don't; it's a skill that you can strengthen over time. Resilience is your key to overcoming obstacles and thriving when faced with adversity.

OVERCOMING OBSTACLES

You are bound to encounter obstacles throughout life. However, it's not the presence of these obstacles that defines you, but rather how you respond to them. Overcoming obstacles reflects our inner strength and resilience.

Imagine obstacles as mountains on your path. Some might be small hills, easy to climb with a little effort, while others might seem impossible to conquer, their peaks lost in the clouds. The size and nature of these mountains vary, but they all serve a purpose in your journey. They teach you patience, perseverance, and the importance of believing in yourself.

When faced with an obstacle, the first step is to acknowledge it. Denying its existence only gives it more power over you. Acknowledge it, but don't give it the power to define your abilities. You are so much more than the challenges you face.

Next, break down the obstacle into smaller, manageable parts. A mountain is climbed one step at a time. Identify the steps you can take to start your ascent. This approach makes the challenge seem less daunting and allows you to celebrate small wins along the way.

Climbing mountains is easier and more enjoyable with companions. Reach out to friends, family, or mentors who can offer support, guidance, or just a listening ear. There's strength in vulnerability, in admitting that you don't have all the answers and need help.

As you overcome each obstacle, take the time to reflect on the journey. What did you learn about yourself? How have you grown? These reflections help you build a resilient mindset and prepare for future challenges. With each obstacle you overcome, your confidence will grow, and what once seemed like insurmountable peaks will become just another part of the landscape of your journey.

Overcoming obstacles is about more than just reaching the other side; it's about the growth within you. Remember, the most beautiful views come after the most demanding climbs. Each obstacle you overcome is a step towards a more resilient and confident you.

LEARNING FROM FAILURE

Failure, as much as it is dreaded, is a powerful teacher. It's a hidden guide that, if listened to, can lead us to paths of unimaginable growth. This section will help you understand how you can learn from your failures to bounce back and leap forward with greater wisdom.

When we talk about failure, we must first change our perspective. Society often paints failure negatively as something to be avoided at all costs. However, the truth is that failure is a natural part of the learning process. It indicates that we are trying, pushing our boundaries, and daring to step out of our comfort zones. Every successful person you admire has faced failure. What sets them apart is their ability to learn from these experiences and not let them define their worth.

Learning from failure starts with accepting it. Acceptance doesn't mean you're okay with failing or don't strive for success. It means acknowledging that failure is a part of your growth journey. When you fail, allow yourself to feel the emotions that come with it—disappointment, frustration, sadness. It's okay to feel these emotions; they make you human. The key is not to dwell on them for too long. Allow yourself to process these feelings, and then, gently but firmly, shift your focus to learning.

Ask yourself, "What can I learn from this experience?" Every failure has a lesson hidden within it. It could be a skill you must develop, a different strategy you must try, or a reminder to be more patient and persistent. Reflecting on these lessons helps you grow stronger. It equips you with the knowledge and insight to face future challenges with a better strategy and mindset.

Sharing your experiences of failure and what you've learned from them can be incredibly empowering. It reminds us that we're not alone in our struggles and that failure is a universal experience. By sharing, we foster community and support, encouraging each other to keep progressing despite setbacks.

Learning from failure also means recognizing when to let go of a particular goal or path. Sometimes, despite our best efforts, things work out differently than we hoped. This doesn't mean you've failed; it means a different path is waiting for you, perhaps better suited to your strengths and passions. Being resilient means being flexible and open to new possibilities when we fail.

HOW TO STAY MOTIVATED

After embracing the lessons learned from failure, we can focus on maintaining a strong motivation. Much like a garden, motivation requires consistent care to flourish. It's the fuel that powers our journey through resilience, pushing us forward even when the path seems steep and unforgiving.

Motivation is not constant; it ebbs and flows like the tide.

There will be days when you feel unstoppable and others when even the simplest tasks seem difficult. This is perfectly normal. The key is not to let the low days define your journey or derail your progress. Instead, use them as moments of rest and reflection, a time to recharge and realign with yourself.

Setting small, achievable goals can help boost your motivation. When you break down your larger aspirations into manageable pieces, each accomplishment becomes a stepping stone toward your ultimate aim.

Another powerful tool for staying motivated is surrounding yourself with positivity. This includes supportive relationships that uplift you and distance yourself from negativity. Seek friends, family members, or mentors who believe in you and your dreams. Their support can be a beacon of light when your motivation falls.

Self-love is the key to staying motivated. Acknowledge your efforts and progress without harsh judgment. Understand that every journey has ups and downs; resilience is built when you respond to challenges.

Visualization can help you maintain motivation. Imagine your future self, having achieved your goals, basking in the glow of your accomplishments. Let this image be a source of inspiration, driving you forward through moments of doubt or hesitation.

Lastly, don't forget to find joy in the journey. Pursue activities that make you happy and fulfilled. Doing this ensures your motivation is fueled by a genuine love for what you do rather than what others want you to do.

CHAPTER SUMMARY

- Resilience is the ability to bounce back from challenges, setbacks, and failures. It's an essential part of personal growth.
- Resilience involves facing difficulties head-on, acknowledging feelings, learning from mistakes, and moving forward positively.
- Building a resilient mindset requires a compassionate inner voice, embracing flexibility, developing problem-solving skills, and having a support network you can rely on.
- Overcoming obstacles teaches us patience, perseverance, and self-belief, with each challenge faced adding to our resilience and confidence.
- Learning from failure is crucial for growth. It involves accepting failure, reflecting on lessons learned, sharing experiences, and being open to new paths.
- Staying motivated is vital to resilience. Setting achievable goals, surrounding yourself with positivity, practicing self-love, and finding joy in the journey can help you stay motivated.
- Resilience and motivation are not natural traits but skills that can be developed over time. They can contribute to a fulfilling journey of self-love and personal growth.

CHAPTER 8
EXPLORING SPIRITUALITY AND INNER PEACE

Spirituality invites you to explore who you are and connect with something greater than yourself. It's about finding meaning, purpose, and peace in your life. For some, spirituality is tied to religion, but it can also be experienced through nature, art, personal growth, and the relationships we form.

Spirituality is about discovering what truly matters to you. It's about understanding your inner world. It encourages you to listen to your heart, find solace in silence, and reach a sense of inner peace that can support you through life's ups and downs.

Spirituality also invites you to explore the beauty of the present moment, practice gratitude, and open your heart to the world's wonders. It's about finding joy in the simple things, learning to let go of what you cannot control, and focusing on what truly brings you peace and fulfillment.

For teen girls, exploring spirituality can be an empowering way to navigate the complexities of growing up. By engaging with your spiritual side, you can learn to appreciate your unique journey and discover a deeper part of yourself you didn't know existed.

There is no right or wrong way to explore your spirituality. It's a path that is unique to you. Whether you find solace in nature, are drawn to meditation and mindfulness, or find inspiration in creative expression, what matters most is that you are taking steps to connect with your inner self and the world around you.

When you explore your spirituality, you open the door to a world of inner peace, self-discovery, and unconditional self-love. It's a journey that will enrich your life and inspire those around you to explore their own paths to inner peace.

FINDING YOUR SPIRITUAL PATH

Discovering your spiritual path involves uncovering what resonates most deeply with you, your values, and your sense of purpose. It's about listening to your heart and allowing it to guide you toward practices and beliefs that bring you closer to your true self.

Finding your spiritual path takes time and an open mindset. It invites you to explore new traditions, practices, and beliefs you may not have considered before. One of the first steps in discovering your spiritual path is to reflect on what spirituality means to you. Consider what makes you feel most connected to something greater than yourself, whether through art, mindfulness, prayer, or acts of kindness. Think about moments when you feel alive, peaceful, and connected. These memories can offer valuable clues to your spiritual path.

Another aspect of finding your spiritual path is to create space for silence and introspection. In a world filled with constant noise and distraction, making time for quiet reflection can help you tune into your inner voice. This could be through yoga or meditation, spending time in nature, or simply sitting quietly with your thoughts. In these moments of stillness, you may find insights about yourself you never knew before.

Don't be afraid to seek out communities or mentors who can support you on your spiritual journey. Connecting with others who share your interests can provide valuable insights, encouragement, and a sense of belonging. Whether it's through online forums, local groups, or mentorship, being part of a community can enrich your spiritual exploration.

PRACTICES FOR INNER PEACE

The following activities can help you connect more deeply with yourself and bring you inner peace, especially if you're looking for an escape from the stresses of teenage life.

Meditation and Mindfulness

Meditation is a powerful tool for achieving inner peace. It allows you to pause, breathe, and connect with the present moment. As a teen girl, your life is filled with changes, challenges, and a constant search for identity. Meditation offers an escape from the noise, where you can listen to your inner voice without judgment. Start with just a few minutes a day, focusing on your breath or a mantra that speaks to you. You can extend this mindfulness to your daily activities, learning to approach life with a sense of calm and presence.

Journaling

Writing down your thoughts and feelings can be very therapeutic. It's a way to express yourself freely and reflect on your experiences. Journaling can help you understand your emotions, celebrate achievements, and learn from your struggles. It's a practice of self-love, acknowledging your journey, and recognizing your worth. You can start by writing about your day, things you're grateful for, or anything on your mind.

Creative Expression

Creativity is a beautiful way to explore your inner world and feelings. Whether through painting, drawing, writing poetry, or playing music, creative activities allow you to channel your emotions in a positive way. They can be a source of joy, relaxation, and a deeper connection with yourself. Don't worry about the outcome; focus on the process and how it makes you feel.

Connecting with Your Body

Your body is your home, and taking care of it is a form of self-love. Practices like yoga, dance, or walking with your pet can help you connect with your body and appreciate its strength and beauty. These activities improve your physical health and mental and emotional well-being. They teach you to listen to your body, honor its needs, and be kind to it.

Spending Time in Silence

Finding moments of silence can be incredibly refreshing in a world that's always buzzing with activity. Silence allows you to turn inward, away from the distractions of the outside world. It's an opportunity to be with yourself, reflect, and find peace. You can spend time in silence by sitting quietly in your room, walking alone, or simply pausing to breathe deeply throughout the day.

These practices are not one-size-fits-all. They are paths for you to explore and find what resonates with you. Approach them with an open mind, allowing yourself to grow and flourish uniquely.

THE ROLE OF NATURE AND SOLITUDE

Did you know that embracing nature and solitude can help you feel more connected to yourself and the world?

Nature offers a unique sense of peace and grounding. It's a reminder of the world's beauty and complexity and how you are a part of this magnificent world. Spending time in nature allows you to step away from the hustle and bustle of daily life, providing a space for reflection and connection with yourself on a deeper level. Whether it's a quiet walk through a park, a moment by the sea, or simply sitting under a tree, these natural experiences can help you feel more connected to the world.

Solitude offers a different kind of peace. In those quiet moments alone, you can genuinely listen to your inner voice, away from the outside world's influence. Solitude provides the space to reflect on your thoughts, feelings, and experiences. It allows you to understand yourself better. It's an opportunity to practice self-care, meditate, read, or simply be with your thoughts.

Combining the healing power of nature with the reflective quality of solitude can change your mental health. It allows you to find peace within yourself and the world, fostering a deeper connection to your inner self.

CONNECTING WITH A HIGHER POWER

Some people find that connecting with a higher power can help them understand their place in the universe and find inner peace. This connection can appear in different ways, depending on your beliefs and experiences. It's about feeling a part of something greater than yourself, which can provide comfort and a sense of belonging.

Connecting with a higher power also involves listening—listening with your ears, heart, and soul. This can be through meditation, prayer, or simply sitting in silence, allowing yourself to feel the presence of something greater. In these moments of quiet and solitude, you can often find the most profound sense of connection and peace.

For many, spirituality is not about adhering strictly to the rituals and teachings of a religion, though it can be for some.

Instead, it's about building an intimate relationship with the essence of life, the universe, or a divine presence.

Discovering your spiritual path is a journey of exploration and reflection. It begins with asking yourself meaningful questions about the nature of existence, the purpose of your life, and the values and principles that guide you.

It's okay not to have all the answers. Spirituality is as much about the questions as it is about the answers. It's about being open to the mystery and wonder of life and learning to trust the journey, even when the destination is unclear.

As you explore your spirituality, you may find that it enriches your life unexpectedly. It can offer a sense of purpose, inspire compassion and empathy, and encourage you to live in alignment with your true self. It can also comfort you during difficult times, reminding you that you are never truly alone.

Embracing spirituality is a powerful step in your journey of self-love. It invites you to look inward and outward with curiosity, connect with the world in a more meaningful way, and find peace in knowing you are a part of something much larger than yourself.

CASE STUDY: ZOE'S QUEST FOR INNER PEACE AND SPIRITUAL CONNECTION

Zoe, a 16-year-old high school student, felt increasingly disconnected from herself and the world around her. Amidst the pressures of academics, social expectations, and life in general, Zoe struggled to find a sense of purpose. She often questioned the deeper meaning of life and her place within it, feeling a void that school and social activities couldn't fill.

One evening, while scrolling through her social media feeds, feeling particularly lost, Zoe stumbled upon a quote about the power of nature and solitude in finding one's true self. This made Zoe wonder how she could find her own inner peace. She decided to embark on a quest to explore her spiritual side and connect with something greater than herself.

Zoe began her journey by dedicating time each morning to sit silently before starting her day. She created a small sanctuary in her room where she could meditate, free from distractions. This mindfulness practice allowed Zoe to start her day with a sense of calm and presence, gradually teaching her the value of living in the moment.

Inspired by her newfound interest in meditation, Zoe sought natural spaces to practice mindfulness and connect with the environment. She started taking long walks in her local park, where she paid close attention to the beauty of the natural world—the sound of the wind rustling through the leaves, the warmth of the sun on her skin, and the peacefulness of the quiet surroundings. These moments in nature became a source of comfort and inspiration for Zoe. It helped her feel grounded and connected to the world in a way she hadn't experienced before.

Zoe also discovered the therapeutic power of journaling. She began writing about her thoughts, feelings, and insights gained during her meditation and nature walks. Journaling became a way for Zoe to process her emotions, celebrate her growth, and reflect on her spiritual journey. Through writing, Zoe started to understand her inner world better and find a sense of inner peace.

Through her exploration of spirituality, Zoe learned the importance of self-love, gratitude, and the beauty of the present moment. She discovered that inner peace comes from within and that connecting with something greater than herself provided a sense of purpose and fulfillment. Zoe's journey changed not just how she viewed the world but also how she saw herself. She realized that her quest for inner peace and spiritual connection was not about finding all the answers but about embracing the journey and trusting the path that unfolded before her.

Zoe's story shows the power of spirituality in finding inner peace and deeper meaning in life. It highlights how mindfulness and nature can help deepen your perception of yourself and the world.

CHAPTER SUMMARY

- Spirituality is a journey of finding meaning, purpose, and inner peace. It's not restricted to religion; it can also be experienced through nature, art, and personal growth.
- Spirituality involves discovering what matters most to you, understanding your inner world, and recognizing the interconnectedness of all things. It encourages you to listen to your heart and find solace in silence.
- Exploring spirituality can empower you to navigate growing up, build self-esteem and self-love, appreciate your unique journey, and embrace imperfections.
- Spirituality encourages living in the present, practicing gratitude, and opening your heart to the world's wonders.
- Finding your spiritual path is an experimental process where you can explore different traditions and practices to connect with your true self.
- Some practices for fostering inner peace include meditation, mindfulness, journaling, creative

expression, connecting with your body, and spending time in silence.
- Nature and solitude can impact your spiritual journey, offering peace, grounding, and space for introspection.
- Connecting with a higher power can help you find comfort, guidance, and a sense of belonging when you feel lost.

CHAPTER 9
SPEAKING UP

Speaking up goes beyond simply being honest with others. It's a way to be true to yourself and honor your feelings, experiences, and perspectives. It's about giving voice to your innermost thoughts and standing firm in your beliefs, even when it's challenging.

Using your voice isn't always easy. It requires courage, strength, and vulnerability. It means opening up about what matters to you, sharing your thoughts and feelings, and not just what you think others want to hear. It's about asserting your needs and desires and respectfully disagreeing when your values don't align with what's being presented.

Why is speaking up so important, especially as a teen girl? Because it's what builds authentic relationships—with yourself and others. When you are honest about who you are, you attract people who appreciate the real you, not just the version of yourself you think others want to see. This authenticity fosters deeper connections that are based on genuine understanding and acceptance.

Using your voice empowers you and reinforces your sense of self-worth and confidence. Each time you voice your thoughts, you affirm your right to have opinions and to take up space in the world. This act of self-affirmation is a powerful form of self-love, as it acknowledges the value of your experiences.

However, speaking your truth also means being prepared for the fact that not everyone will agree with you or support your perspective. And that's okay. Disagreement does not reduce the validity of your feelings or experiences. It reminds us that diversity of thought makes life rich and complex. Learning to navigate these differences is part of the process.

Your voice reflects your inner world, and using it wisely can lead to meaningful change. Your voice matters. Your experiences, thoughts, and feelings deserve to be heard. Speaking up is not just about vocalizing your inner world; it's an act of self-love that empowers you.

THE POWER OF NO

Using your voice is also about knowing when and how to assert your boundaries. This brings us to a simple yet powerful word: "No."

"No" is a complete sentence. It doesn't require justification, explanation, or apology. But for many of us, especially in our teenage years, saying no can be tricky. We worry about disappointing others, being perceived as rude, or missing out. However, embracing the power of "No" is essential for our mental health and self-respect.

When you say no to something that doesn't align with your values, drains your energy, or doesn't feel right, you are honoring your needs and priorities. It's a declaration that you understand and respect your limits. This act of self-care sends a powerful message to yourself and others about your self-worth.

Saying no can also open doors. When you decline commitments that don't serve you, you create space in your life for experiences, relationships, and opportunities that do. This space allows you to engage more fully with what truly matters and makes you happy.

Learning to say no with confidence is a skill that takes practice. Start small, with low-stakes situations, and gradually work your way up. Pay attention to how you feel when you assert your boundaries. It might be uncomfortable at first, but it will become more natural with time. Remember, your feelings and needs are valid. You have the right to protect your time, energy, and well-being.

As you become more comfortable with saying no, you'll find that your ability to advocate for yourself and others strengthens. You'll be better equipped to stand up for your beliefs, support causes that matter to you, and contribute to positive change. When it's aligned with your values, saying no is an act of courage and self-love.

Embracing the power of "No" is a transformative step in your journey toward self-love. As you continue to empower your voice, remember that every no opens the path to a yes that resonates more deeply with who you are and aspire to be.

ADVOCATING FOR YOURSELF AND OTHERS

Advocating means standing up for yourself and lending your voice to those who might not have the strength or platform to do so. It's about harnessing the power of your voice in a way that respects yourself and others.

Advocating for yourself starts with understanding your worth. It's okay to ask for what you need, whether it's support, space, or respect. Asserting yourself doesn't mean being selfish or demanding; it means being true to yourself and honoring your needs and boundaries.

When it comes to advocating for others, it's about empathy and action. It's seeing someone in a situation where they're not being heard or respected and choosing to stand with them. This could be as simple as supporting a friend going through a tough time or speaking out against injustice in your community. Advocacy is about using your voice for good, uplifting and supporting others, and creating a ripple effect of positive change.

Advocating for yourself and others isn't always easy. It requires courage and resilience, especially when faced with opposition or indifference. But remember, every time you choose to speak up, you're not only empowering yourself but also paving the way for others to do the same. It's about creating a culture of respect and kindness where everyone's voice matters.

As you continue to navigate the complexities of adolescence and beyond, remember that your voice is a powerful tool for change. Whether in personal relationships, within your school, or in the broader community, never underestimate the impact you can make. By advocating for yourself and others, you're contributing to a world where everyone is seen, heard, and valued. And that, in itself, is a beautiful act of self-love and empowerment.

PUBLIC SPEAKING AND COMMUNICATION SKILLS

One of the most transformative skills you can develop is the ability to communicate effectively and confidently in public settings. Public speaking and communication are not just about making speeches or presentations; they're about expressing your thoughts and beliefs in a way that impacts others. This skill is a powerful extension of advocating for yourself and others, allowing you to share your voice and impact the world.

Feeling nervous about public speaking is entirely normal. Even the most experienced speakers feel a flutter of nerves before stepping onto the stage. The key is not to eliminate these feelings but to learn to harness them as a source of energy and passion for your message.

First, let's focus on the basis of effective communication: authenticity. When you speak from a place of authenticity, your words carry more weight and sincerity. This means being true to yourself, your values, and your message. It's about showing up as the real you, not a version you think people want to see. When you are authentic, your audience can connect with you on a deeper level, making your message more impactful.

Clarity is the next pillar of effective public speaking. Clarity in communication means being concise and direct, ensuring your message is understood. This involves organizing your thoughts beforehand and choosing your words carefully. A clear message is powerful because it leaves little room for misunderstanding, allowing your audience to grasp your perspective fully.

Another vital aspect of public speaking is engaging your audience. This can be achieved through storytelling, asking rhetorical questions, or even incorporating humor where appropriate. Engagement is about creating a two-way communication stream, even if the audience isn't speaking back. It's about making them feel involved, valued, and considered.

Lastly, practice is paramount. Like any other skill, the more you practice public speaking, the more comfortable and confident you become. Start small by sharing your thoughts in a more intimate setting, like a family dinner or a discussion with friends. As your confidence grows, seek out larger platforms to share your voice. Every great speaker starts somewhere; every opportunity to speak is a step toward mastering this empowering skill.

As you continue to develop your public speaking and communication skills, remember that your voice can inspire change, advocate for justice, and connect with others. By embracing this power, you are empowering yourself and paving the way for others to find their voices.

LEAVING A LEGACY

Your legacy is the impact your voice can have on the world. Your voice is not just a tool for expressing thoughts or commanding attention; it's a powerful instrument for change. This section explores what it means to leave a legacy through the power of your voice and how you, as a young woman, can harness this to make a meaningful impact.

Leaving a legacy is about creating something that outlives you and continues to inspire, empower, and guide others even when you're not physically present. It's about using your voice to plant seeds of change and hope in those around you and those who will come after you. Your legacy is the mark you leave on the world, a reflection of the lives you've touched and the difference you've made.

Start by reflecting on the values and causes that are important to you. What issues spark a fire in your heart? Is it advocating for mental health awareness, fighting for gender equality, or championing environmental conservation? Identifying your passions is the first step towards using your voice in a way that aligns with your values.

Once you've pinpointed these areas of passion, consider the platforms through which you can amplify your voice. In today's digital age, there are countless ways to make your voice heard, from social media and blogging to community volunteering and public speaking events. Each platform offers a unique opportunity to reach different audiences.

Leaving a legacy is not just about the scale of your impact but also about the depth of it. It's about the personal connections you forge, the lives you touch in meaningful ways, and the inspiration you inspire others to find their voices.

You will need to embrace resilience and perseverance on this journey. You will face challenges and setbacks, but it's through these experiences that your voice will become even more impactful. Each obstacle is an opportunity to learn, grow, and refine your vision for the legacy you wish to leave.

By empowering your voice with purpose and passion, you're not just leaving a legacy but shaping the future. So, speak up, speak out, and let your voice be a beacon of change, hope, and empowerment for future generations.

CHAPTER SUMMARY

- Self-love involves learning to speak up and honoring your feelings, experiences, and perspectives.
- Speaking your truth requires courage and vulnerability and allows you to assert your needs and set boundaries.
- Authenticity in expressing yourself helps form deeper connections with others and reinforces your self-worth and confidence.
- Embracing the power of "No" is crucial for your mental health, self-respect, and personal growth.
- Advocating for yourself and others involves standing up for rights, beliefs, and needs and using your voice for positive change.
- Developing public speaking and communication skills empowers you and enhances your ability to express your thoughts and beliefs to others.
- You can use your voice to inspire, empower, and guide others, creating a lasting impact and legacy.

CHAPTER 10
NAVIGATING CHANGE

Change is as inevitable in life as the rising and setting of the sun. It's a constant companion, sometimes arriving as a gentle breeze and, at other times, as a turbulent storm.

Change is the process of becoming different. This might sound simple, but its impact on your life can be profound and far-reaching. It can affect your relationships, self-image, goals, and even dreams. But here's the thing: change also brings growth, learning, and self-discovery, especially during your teenage years.

Understanding change begins with acknowledging that it is a natural part of life. Just as the seasons shift in a never-ending cycle, so too do the phases of your life. Each transition you face is not just an end but a beginning, offering new opportunities for you to grow and explore who you are. Whether starting a new school, moving to a different city, or navigating friendships and relationships, each change teaches you to adapt and learn.

One of the most empowering steps you can take is to welcome change with an open heart and mind. This doesn't mean it's always easy, or you won't face moments of doubt and uncertainty. It's natural to feel a mix of emotions when confronted with change. You might feel excited about the new opportunities ahead and anxious about leaving the familiar behind. These feelings are a normal part of the process; acknowledging them is the first step toward moving forward.

Everyone experiences change, and seeking support from family, friends, or mentors is okay. Sharing your thoughts and feelings can help you process your emotions and gain insights from the experiences of others. Practicing self-care is crucial during times of change. Taking care of your physical, emotional, and mental well-being can help you stay grounded in the face of uncertainty.

Understanding change involves recognizing that you have the power to shape how you respond to it. While you might not have control over every aspect of a transition, you do have control over your attitude and actions. By approaching change with a positive mindset and a willingness to learn, you can turn challenges into opportunities for growth. How you choose to navigate these transitions can shape the person you become.

EMBRACING NEW BEGINNINGS

As we journey through the winding paths of adolescence, we encounter moments that feel like standing at the edge of a new horizon. These moments are full of potential but often accompanied by uncertainty. Embracing new beginnings is not just about stepping forward into the unknown; it's about recognizing the strength within ourselves that makes each step possible.

New beginnings can take many forms. It may be starting a new school year, forging a new friendship, or discovering a hobby that sets your soul alight. Each offers a unique opportunity to learn more about who you are and who you aspire to be. It's a time to listen to your heart and trust your ability to navigate the journey ahead.

New beginnings give you a chance to redefine yourself. You are not bound by past perceptions or limitations. Instead, you can explore different facets of your personality, experiment with new interests, and grow in ways you never thought possible. Remember, self-love is at the core of this exploration. It's about allowing yourself to try, fail, and try again while knowing that you are worthy of love with every change that comes your way.

It's natural to feel a mix of excitement and apprehension. Accept these feelings as signs that you are alive and only human. Lean into the support of friends, family, and mentors who can offer guidance and encouragement. And remember to be that source of support for others, too. Shared experiences can deepen connections and provide comfort during times of change.

Change doesn't happen overnight, and challenges and

setbacks often accompany growth. Be gentle with yourself and learn from every experience.

HOW TO DEAL WITH LOSS AND GRIEF

In our lives, we are bound to encounter moments that challenge our strength and test our ability to stand back up after being knocked down. Dealing with loss and grief is one of the most overwhelming experiences that can impact our well-being. It's a universal part of the human experience. Still, it can feel isolating, especially during our teenage years when every emotion is magnified.

Loss is not just about the death of a loved one. It can also mean the end of a friendship, changing family dynamics, moving away from a place we call home, or even losing a part of ourselves that we cherish.

Grief is our emotional response to loss. It can appear in various ways—sadness, anger, confusion, or even numbness. It's important to understand that all these feelings are normal. They are not signs of weakness but indicators of our love and connection for what we've lost.

During these times, self-love becomes more important than ever. It's about permitting yourself to feel whatever you're feeling without criticism. It's about recognizing the strength within you, even when you feel most vulnerable. Some days will be better than others, and that's okay.

Here are a few steps to help you navigate through loss and grief.

Allow Yourself to Feel

Trying to bottle up your emotions or pretending they don't exist can lead to more pain in the long run. Allow yourself time to grieve, cry, or simply sit with your feelings.

Express Your Emotions

Whether it's through journaling, art, music, or talking with someone you trust, find a way to express what you're going through. Expression can be a powerful tool for healing.

Seek Support

Remember, you don't have to go through this alone. Lean on friends, family, or a support group where you can share your feelings and experiences with others who understand what you're going through.

Take Care of Yourself

Grief can take a toll on your physical well-being. Try to maintain a routine that includes proper nutrition, sleep, and physical activity. It's not about perfection but making small choices that honor your body and mind.

Find Moments of Joy

It might feel impossible initially, but try to find moments of joy in your daily life. It could be something as simple as listening to music, spending time with friends, or playing with a pet. These moments are not about forgetting your loss but about finding a balance.

Remember and Honor

Find a way to remember and honor the person, relationship, or part of yourself that you've lost. This could be through a memory book, a personal ritual, or a creative project. Honoring your loss can be a step towards healing.

Surrounding ourselves with understanding and compassionate people can provide a safe space to navigate our emotions and gradually find our footing again. The goal is not to move on from our loss but to learn to live with it, allowing us to feel a sense of peace and ease.

THE ROLE OF SUPPORT SYSTEMS

Support systems are invaluable during your teenage years. As you navigate life's changes, whether related to school, relationships, or personal identity, the people around you - friends, family, mentors, and even communities - play a pivotal role in how you perceive and tackle these changes.

A support system is not just a safety net for when things go wrong; it's a network of people that fosters your growth, resilience, and self-esteem. It's about having people who lift you up during your lowest moments. These individuals provide a mirror to your inner world, reflecting the strength and beauty you may not always see in yourself.

Building these relationships requires effort and intention. It's about choosing to surround yourself with positivity and genuine care. This doesn't mean that every person in your life will always understand what you're going through. However, it's about having at least one person who truly listens to your thoughts and feelings without judgment.

As we've explored in earlier chapters, a support system can also mean seeking professional help when needed. There's strength in recognizing when you need guidance beyond what your immediate circle can provide. Therapists, counselors, and other mental health professionals can offer invaluable perspectives and tools to help you navigate your emotions and experiences.

The quality of your support system is far more important than the quantity. It's about depth, not breadth. Having a few close, meaningful relationships is more beneficial than having numerous superficial connections. These deep bonds provide a sense of security and belonging, essential ingredients for self-love and acceptance.

As you move forward, remember that leaning on others is okay. Independence is a valuable trait, but interdependence—the ability to be independent while also relying on and supporting others—is a strength. Life's transitions become more manageable when you have a support system to share your joys, sorrows, and everything in between.

LOOKING FORWARD WITH HOPE

As you journey through your teens, you'll find yourself at the crossroads of numerous transitions. These moments, filled with changes and challenges, can sometimes cloud your vision with uncertainty. As we move from understanding the importance of support systems, let's shift our focus towards looking forward with hope, an equally important aspect of navigating life's transitions.

Hope is not just a feeling. It's a choice to believe in the possibility of a brighter tomorrow despite the current circumstances. It's about holding onto the light, even when the night is dark. For you, as a teen girl learning to embrace self-love, hope can be your guiding star. It can help you see beyond the immediate hurdles and recognize the endless possibilities that lie ahead.

To cultivate hope, start by setting small, achievable goals for yourself. These goals don't have to be monumental; they just need to be meaningful to you. It could be improving a skill, making a new friend, or even learning to appreciate your own company more. Achieving these goals will boost your confidence and reinforce your belief in your ability to influence your future positively.

Another way to foster hope is to practice gratitude. When we're focused on what's going wrong, it's easy to overlook the good in our lives. Take a moment each day to reflect on things you're thankful for, no matter how small. This practice can shift your perspective, helping you see the light in the midst of darkness and encouraging a hopeful outlook.

Hope is also about resilience. It's about getting back up when life knocks you down and learning from each experience. Every challenge you face is an opportunity to grow stronger and wiser. Embrace these moments, not with fear, but with the courage to believe you have what it takes to overcome them.

Looking forward with hope is not about denying the difficulties of today. It's about believing in the promise of tomorrow. It's about seeing yourself for who you are now and who you can become. As you navigate life's transitions, let hope guide you toward a future filled with endless possibilities.

CHAPTER SUMMARY

- Change is a natural and inevitable part of life, affecting various aspects such as relationships, self-image, and goals. It also offers opportunities for growth and self-discovery.
- Try to embrace change with an open heart and mind, even though it may bring a mix of emotions like excitement and anxiety.
- Seeking support from family, friends, or mentors and practicing self-care can help you better navigate change
- You can shape your response to change by adopting a positive mindset and a willingness to learn. This attitude can turn challenges into opportunities for growth.
- New beginnings present opportunities to learn more about yourself, redefine your identity, and embrace self-love.
- Dealing with loss and grief is part of the human experience. It requires allowing yourself to feel, seeking support, and finding moments of joy.
- A solid support system, including friends, family, mentors, and professional help, plays a pivotal role in personal growth, resilience, and self-esteem during the transitions of your teenage years.
- Cultivating hope through setting small goals, practicing gratitude, and surrounding yourself with positivity can help you navigate life's challenges and look forward to a future filled with possibilities.

YOUR SELF-LOVE JOURNEY

As you stand at this moment, on the brink of the rest of your life, take a moment to pause and reflect on the ideas we've explored together in this book. The path to self-love and embracing your spark is not the same for everyone.

It's a deeply personal voyage that has seen you navigate the calm and the storm, learning and growing with every step.

Think back to the moments of doubt and uncertainty, when loving yourself felt like an impossible challenge. These times tested your resilience and ability to stand firm in the face of adversity. But you persevered, armed with the knowledge and the tools you've gathered along the way. Each challenge is an opportunity to learn more about yourself and understand your needs, desires, and the incredible strength within you.

Remember the moments of triumph and joy, the milestones that marked progress on your journey. These are the times when self-love feels like a natural state, when you can see your worth and value reflected in the world around you. These moments are just as crucial to your journey because they remind you what you're working towards—a life where self-love has a permanent place in your heart.

There may be setbacks, such as when you stumble or fall short of your expectations. But with each of these moments comes the opportunity to practice self-compassion and treat yourself with the same kindness and understanding you would offer to a close friend. This, too, is an essential component of self-love because it allows you to celebrate your imperfections and recognize that they do not define your worth.

The journey of self-love is an ongoing one. There will always be new challenges to face and new lessons to learn. But you are now equipped with amazing tools that foster self-awareness, self-compassion, and resilience. You understand that self-love is not a destination but a continuous path. It's a path you will walk with confidence, grace, and an unwavering belief in your worth.

As you move forward, carry with you the lessons of the past, the joy of the present, and the hope for the future. Remember that self-love is your birthright, a legacy that you will continue to build with each day. It is the light that guides you through the darkness, the anchor that holds you steady in the storm.

So, take a moment to celebrate yourself and all that you've achieved. You are a work in progress, a masterpiece unfolding with each new chapter of your life. As you continue on this journey, know that you are not alone. You are part of a community of strong, resilient individuals walking this path alongside you, each of us striving towards a world where self-love is not just a dream but a reality.

THE CONTINUOUS PATH OF SELF-LOVE

The path of self-love does not have a definitive end. It's a continuous journey, unfolding with each step, offering new lessons and challenges that help you grow.

Self-love is an evolving practice that requires patience, understanding, and, most importantly, kindness toward yourself. It's about acknowledging your worth and value, even when you feel less than perfect.

Remember, perfection is not the goal; growth is. Each day presents a new opportunity to practice self-love, make choices that reflect your worth, and treat yourself with the same compassion you offer others.

As you continue on this path, you'll find that self-love becomes the basis upon which you build your life. It influences the decisions you make, the relationships you form, and the dreams you pursue. It becomes a source of strength and confidence, empowering you to face challenges with the right attitude and strength.

Allow yourself to explore new passions, step outside your comfort zone, and embrace the person you are becoming.

INSPIRING OTHERS

Your experience has the power to light the way for others. Your narrative is unique and holds universal truths about the human experience. The moments of doubt, leaps of faith, quiet mornings spent in reflection, and joyful discoveries of self-worth are chapters in a story many are waiting to hear. When you open up about loving yourself, you permit others to do the same. You show them it's okay to be imperfect, struggle, and grow.

Imagine a world where every young girl knows her worth, where she understands that her value is not dependent on the opinions of others or the number on a scale. By sharing your story, you contribute to this vision. You become a part of a larger narrative of empowerment and self-acceptance. Your voice, experiences, and insights become part of the collective wisdom that guides the next generation toward a kinder, more compassionate relationship with themselves.

Be authentic and honest when sharing your story. The most powerful stories are those told from the heart, without ego or embellishment. Your vulnerability is your strength. It connects you to others in profound and meaningful ways. It reminds us all that we all struggle or search for love and acceptance.

Your story can comfort someone who feels isolated in their experiences. It can challenge societal norms that dictate how we should look, think, or feel. Most importantly, it can inspire others to begin their own journeys of self-love and love themselves fully and unconditionally.

Your self-love legacy is not just about the relationship you've formed with yourself; it's also about how you use your journey to illuminate the paths of others. It's a legacy of kindness, courage, and connection—a reminder that we are all beautifully flawed, infinitely valuable, and deeply connected in our shared human experience.

COMMITTING TO LIFELONG GROWTH

Self-love is about embracing every part of who you are at every stage of your life and recognizing that growth is not only possible but essential.

Committing to lifelong growth means recognizing that the person you are today is not the final version of yourself. It's about permitting yourself to evolve, make mistakes, and learn from them. It's about understanding that every experience, whether good or bad, is an opportunity for growth and self-discovery.

This commitment can be challenging. It requires courage, resilience, and an unwavering belief in yourself. It means stepping out of your comfort zone, challenging your beliefs, and embracing the unknown with open arms. Within you lies an infinite well of strength and wisdom. You can overcome any obstacle, reach any height, and become the person you were always meant to be.

A FINAL MESSAGE

As we draw the curtains on this journey together, I want to leave you with a final message that I hope will resonate with you for years to come. This message is one of love and empowerment.

You are a work in progress. Every experience, lesson you've learned, and step towards loving yourself more deeply has added another stroke of beauty to your canvas.

As you move through life, know that the path to self-love will have ups and downs. There will be days when loving yourself feels effortless and days when it feels like the hardest thing in the world. On those tough days, I want you to remember this: You are not alone. You are part of a community of incredible women who are all on their own journeys of self-discovery and self-love. Lean on this community, share your stories, and let the strength of others lift you up when you need it most.

I also want to remind you that self-love is a radical act of empowerment. Choosing to love yourself just as you are is a powerful statement in a world that often tries to dictate how we should look, think, and feel. It's a declaration that you are enough, worthy of love and respect and have the right to take up space in this world.

So, as you close this book and step back into your life, I encourage you to carry these messages with you. Let them be your guiding light as you continue to grow, evolve, and become the most authentic version of yourself.

Remember, this is just the beginning of your self-love journey. And I am confident that you will create a beautiful, empowering legacy of self-love that will inspire others for generations to come.

Thank you for allowing me to be a part of your journey. Here's to your self-love legacy—a legacy that is uniquely and wonderfully yours.

EPILOGUE

As we close the pages of this book, remember that your journey to self-love and confidence is ongoing, filled with ups and downs, triumphs and challenges. Armed with the guidance, insights, and tips you've gathered through this collection, you are now better equipped to navigate the complexities of teenage life with self-awareness and a deep sense of self-worth.

The path to embracing your true self is uniquely yours. There will be days filled with joy and others where doubts may creep in. It's all part of the beautiful, intricate process of growing up.

As you continue your journey, let the stories, advice, and strategies from these books guide you toward a life where self-love and confidence are not just aspirations but reality. Embrace your journey with an open heart, a curious mind, and the unwavering belief that you are enough, just as you are.

In today's fast-paced, ever-changing world, the lessons of self-assurance, resilience, and self-compassion are more valuable than ever. Carry them with you as you forge your path, knowing that the ultimate destination is not perfection but continuous self-discovery and growth.

Thank you for allowing me to be a part of your journey. May you move forward with the ability to face whatever comes your way, the resilience to bounce back from setbacks, and the love for yourself that shines brightly for the world to see.

Here's to thriving in your teens, embracing your spark, and stepping into the world with confidence and self-love. The future is bright, and it begins with you.

YOUR FEEDBACK MATTERS

As we reach the end of this book, I extend my heartfelt gratitude for your time and engagement. It's been an honor to share this journey with you, and I hope it has been as enriching for you as it has been for me.

Your feedback helps me as an independent author and guides fellow readers searching for their next meaningful read. Your insights and reflections are invaluable; by sharing them, you contribute to a larger conversation that extends far beyond the pages of this book.

If the ideas we've explored have sparked new thoughts, inspired change, or provided comfort, I'd really appreciate it if you could share your experience with others by leaving a review on the platform on which you purchased this book.

Thank you once again for your company on this literary adventure. May the insights you've gained stay with you, and may your quest for knowledge be ever-fulfilling.

ABOUT THE AUTHOR

Ella Bradley is an educator and author, specializing in the development and empowerment of teenagers. With a rich background in child and teenager education, Ella has dedicated her career to equipping young minds with the knowledge and skills they need to navigate life successfully.

Her passion for education extends beyond the classroom and into her writing, where she addresses critical topics such as personal finance, career planning, and mental health. Ella's books are renowned for their practicality, clarity, and engaging style, making complex concepts accessible and enjoyable for teenagers.

Through her insightful and comprehensive books, Ella has helped countless teenagers take control of their futures. Whether she's teaching in a classroom or writing a book, her goal remains the same: to help teenagers grow into confident, capable adults.

ALSO BY ELLA BRADLEY

Ultimate Guide to Personal Finance for Teens

Ultimate Guide to Career Planning for Teens

Teen's Guide to Future Success

www.ingramcontent.com/pod-product-compliance
Lightning Source LLC
Chambersburg PA
CBHW052134070526
44585CB00017B/1818